ATHEISM

DEBUNKED

First published in Great Britain by
L.R. Price Publications Ltd, 2021.

This edition published by
L.R. Price Publications Ltd.,
27 Old Gloucester Street,
London, WC1N 3AX
www.lrpricepublications.com

ISBN: 9781838061081

ATHEISM

DEBUNKED

Duncan Kilburn

Contents

1. Introduction..

2. History of the scientific explanation of the Universe..

3. The Mathematical basis of the laws of nature................

4. The Fine-Tuning Problem (FTP)............................

5. The Quantum Measurement Problem (QMP).................

6. The Counterarguments to FTP and QMP......................

    6.1 The 'Multiverse' concept – a counter argument to FTP..

    6.2 The theistic creation dilemma: 'if God created the Universe, then who in turn created God?'...............

    6.3 The 'intelligence must emerge late' concept.............

    6.4 Why not solipsism?.....................................

    6.5 The paradox of the quantum 'Universal locking problem'...

7. Discussion of other challenging areas of science

    7.1 Darwinian evolution....................................

    7.2 The karyotype problem.................................

    7.3 The biological chirality problem...........................

    7.4 Darwinian evolution (Continued).........................

    7.5 The consciousness problem.............................

    7.6 The matter/anti-matter symmetry problem..............

8. Summary...

9. Afterword..

10. Appendix 1...

11. Appendix 2...

12. Glossary..

13. Index...

1. Introduction

Sir Isaac Newton:

"...all material things seem to have been composed of the hard and solid particles... variously associated with the first Creation by the counsel of an Intelligent Agent..."

Propaganda is very effective. If you repeat a lie often enough, a large proportion of the population will come to believe it in time. Atheism and secularism currently seem to hold an ever-greater grip on our society, popular culture, politics and the wider media. Yet in the parallel world of science, atheism has in fact arguably lost a great deal of ground, both evidentially and philosophically, in recent years. This is primarily the consequence of the groundbreaking scientific discoveries made over the course of the last few decades. There is a strong sense now amongst some that a popular recourse now needs to be made against the seemingly prevailing contrary opinion. Nietzsche once claimed, 'God is dead'; reports of his 'demise' have, however, been greatly exaggerated. In fact, there is arguably now more rational reason to accept the existence of God than at any time in human history, but not necessarily in any religious context. The purpose of this book is to sow seeds of doubt in virtually everything you have ever been likely told, taught, advised and influenced by. The philosophers and sages throughout history have, as always, advised you to question everything you've ever been told. No matter who said it, no matter if they said it and indeed no matter if you said it to yourself.

So why then do people so readily trust the opinions of any given era of time? Or any period of history as though it was cornerstone of all knowledge and wisdom? That, of course, has never been found to be the case, ever. In spite of all the usual unabated enthusiasm of the given supporters of the great fashionable thought of any given period. Has any era in human history ever been found to have the final word? Will it ever? Does modern science hold a greater truth and accuracy that what had been known before? Many (including the author) certainly think it does. If so, why then are so many of the true revelations of current scientific understanding essentially being ignored in the modern popular discourse? There is a real sense that this is an era where intellectual thinking has gone completely awry. The dominant narrative of modern times is arguably as dubious, if not more so, as in any period in history, but it's totally infused with its own predictable overconfidence and its belief in its own 'correctness and finality'. Ironically, the roots of this current narrative actually emerged from early modern science, which was, of course, based entirely on the opposite mindset, seeking and understanding the certainties of a 'divinely created logical Universe'.

Similarly, you'll often hear arguments pertaining to the so-called 'scientific consensus', as somehow a countenance to any questioning voice. That to disagree with the current 'consensus' is somehow a 'negative' thing to do. Since when has science had anything to do with consensus? Science is about pushing the boundaries at all times and questioning everything without exception. Skepticism is a scientist's vocation. In the Middle Ages and prior, for example, the overwhelming scientific consensus was that the Earth was at the center of the Universe – they weren't correct. In reality, a great deal of the portrayed 'truth' is little more than mere current academic fashion. You do not win Nobel prizes by promoting the constraints contained within the current dogma. But rather by a great discovery, triggering a seismic paradigm shift within science. Clearly, historically some shifts are greater than others, but all hold to the same effect.

The discussion of anything which may mix perceived metaphysical concepts with 'mainstream' science is certainly to some a degree a taboo subject. But at times the need to popularize the 'unfashionable' arises out of the need to establish where human knowledge and understanding at any one point actually stands. This is certainly not a book about religion, though it does arguably support rational theism. It is primarily a discussion about a very provocative current debate in modern science, particularly within the realms of physics and cosmology.

Nor is this book in any way focused on discussing Darwinist evolution, which is a commonly debated subject area that is mentioned in the later chapters. Initially, the Darwinist concept of evolution within a given species (micro-evolution) is clearly a well-established concept which is supported by a great deal of evidence. However, further into the book such concepts known as the 'karyotype problem', the 'chirality problem' and the utter paucity of transitional forms found in the fossil record will be discussed. These are experimentally well-observed phenomena that seriously question the scientific validity of the wider claims commonly ascribed to Darwinian evolution. In spite of this, how often is this heard or discussed in the popular arena? You'll often still encounter many naturalist arguments made in relation to atheism based entirely on biological principles and in particular Darwinist evolution alone. This is often presented as though biology single-handedly is sufficient to resolve the debate on whether a 'creator of the Universe exists or not'. This is rather strange given that, in reality, biology deals with a very 'high-level' aspect of the natural world. Given its existence and functioning relies entirely on the underlying chemistry and physics involved in the first place. Physics essentially underpins everything in science, and this is therefore why the true debate hangs primarily around physics alone – without physics there would be no biology (or chemistry for that matter). Physics is fundamental; biology is not.

In recent times there appears to have grown a militant strand of naturalist/atheist thinking that has sought to appropriate science entirely as its own. Therefore, using the authority of science to legitimize naturalism and atheism as though it is a scientifically proven concept. In the UK, Professor Richard Dawkins is probably the most famous proponent of this mindset, but there are many who hold and popularize these views. Thanks to such commentators, it could be argued that it has become increasingly difficult to raise challenging questions and expose fundamental flaws in much of modern scientific knowledge without religion being instantly raised within the debate as little more than a strawman diversion.

When debating anyone scientifically, it's usually highly informative initially to ask them on what their understanding/definition of the scientific method actually is. It is commonly to be found that those who doggedly hold on to opinions such as naturalism, environmentalism and Darwinism are almost universally what's known in the trade as 'naïve inductivists'. They possess and share a commonly held naïve view of science that is basically little more than drawing lines on graphs and seeking ever more 'data confirmation points'. This is how most assuredly science does NOT work. The mature, detailed and accurate view of the scientific method is based on hard experimentally driven deduction by means of 'conjecture and refutation', as best exemplified by the work of the great modern philosopher Sir Karl Popper (1902-1994). Taken with that insight in mind, it is actually quite easy to poke holes into the many popular pseudo-sciences of modern times, the previously mentioned trio being a case in point.

Contrary to their meaning in everyday language, 'proving' and 'disproving' are very different things and are logically highly asymmetric. Repeated confirming observations of an idea (e.g. 'all swans are white') fundamentally proves nothing; you may be confident in that statement but it simply means you haven't as yet found a possible refutation (i.e. 'a black swan'). However, observation of a single confirmed refutation event utterly obliterates the original idea (i.e. 'black swan(s) do exist in Australia'). Refuting data is vastly more powerful logically than any accrued confirming data. One confirmed refutation data point blows any theory to pieces even if there were previously a trillion 'confirmation' data points gathered. Confirmation data might demonstrate a theory has value, but it fundamentally proves nothing. That's how science really works; induction is the methodology of pseudo-science, whilst deduction is the methodology of true science.

In the bubble of truth, there reside only two valid statements:

1. Ideas/theories which have so far survived falsification testing.

2. Ideas/theories which have not survived falsification testing.

Perhaps other than pure mathematics (which is also equally highly debatable) no truth lies outside these two statements; everything else is based on faith and faith alone – and that is a good thing, not a bad thing. The scientific method is more predicated on faith than just about any other concept in human thought. Faith is simply holding optimism in the seemingly self-evident truth, without being able to completely prove it. The underlying premises of the scientific method are a picture-perfect example of this mindset.

The reason why the notion that the Earth being at the center of the Universe was the scientific consensus for thousands of years is precisely because no one had as yet then found any falsification data for it. This being in clear contrast to the commonly held evidence that the Earth was indeed at the center of the Universe, with all motion in relation to it. However, when Galileo pointed his new telescope at Jupiter in 1610 and spotted four moons in orbit around it, thousands of years of scientific consensus was shattered in a blink of an eye. Inductivists cannot explain why within the history of science so many ideas which were held up so firmly as 'scientific facts' for countless years, then ended up being completely debunked and cast off. Deductivists, in stark contrast, can explain the mistakes and history of science in one sentence: a theory survives until confirmed data refutes it – most theories (if not all) will ultimately be overthrown. Crucially, when a theory is refuted, the prior 'confirmation data' does not somehow magically evaporate or disappear, but the theory remains destroyed.

This understanding is often not to be found in either popular or much of modern academic discourse yet will be utilized many times throughout this book. Such as the Human/Chimpanzee Y chromosome divergence data discussed later, etc. Which, in that particular example, arguably refutes any notion of 'recent common ancestry' between those two species. But in contrast, how often do you hear Darwinists claiming, 'there's so much evidence in favor of evolution'?

The assumption that naturalism is the default understanding of science is to an ever-greater extent widely portrayed. But does the world of science (and particularly physics and cosmology) so neatly fit into this naturalist/atheist view of the Universe? In fact, the flow and orientation of modern science is actually very much against the tide of naturalism and atheism seen in so much of modern culture, contrary to what is often portrayed. Those who seek to lazily conflate science with naturalism and atheism can be quite readily shown to be, in fact, on very questionable scientific and philosophical ground indeed.

The fundamental purpose of this book is therefore to ask a specific question in simple terms: does science actually imply or support atheism? To attempt to answer this difficult problem, it will be argued that an answer can be given to it by rephrasing it in the following form: has modern science uncovered evidence about the physical Universe that *cannot* be explained or described in purely naturalistic or materialistic terms (which are commonly taken to innately imply atheism)?

The argument has two clear underlying assumptions:

1. The Universe had a definite temporal beginning – therefore a scientific explanation of the origin of the Universe is actually required in the first place.

2. Naturalism inherently implies atheism, given that naturalism denies any teleological or supernatural input into nature – therefore anything which doubts naturalism, immediately by implication doubts atheism.

The key modern scientific realization that the Universe did indeed have a definite temporal origin is discussed in the following chapter of this book. This discovery is found to be pivotal to the main argument and is discussed both in terms of its historical context as well as the technical and experimental basis of the idea.

The following chapters seek to outline the key arguments and the scientific discoveries involved, which will hopefully draw the reader to question many of the popular assumptions and general narrative that they may have become accustomed to.

The principal arguments revolve around two distinct concepts known to modern physics and cosmology, which have come to be appreciated by scientists over the course of the last century. Firstly coming from the fundamental physics of quantum mechanics, a concept knows as the Quantum Measurement Problem (QMP) and secondly, the other coming primarily from the realm of cosmology known as the Fine-Tuning Problem (FTP). The strength of this debate has increased significantly over the past couple of decades because of new discoveries in the realm of cosmology in particular. The ramifications of these discoveries, it is fair to say, have created a certain unease within the academic realm because of their startling possible conclusions. Later chapters discuss other areas such as consciousness, the notion of free-will and evolution. The clear demarcation between the methodology of science versus the ideology of naturalism is importantly maintained in the underlying context throughout.

2. History of the scientific explanation of the Universe

Sir Karl Popper:

"...true ignorance is not the absence of knowledge but the refusal to acquire it...

...a theory that explains everything, explains nothing..."

A scientific description of the origin of the Universe has become the focus and a primary source of discussion and debate over the course of the last century. This is particularly remarkable as for most of the history of science the Universe was generally thought to be eternal and without a beginning – precisely that it had no origin. This was a source of much chagrin to many philosophers and theologians who had in previous centuries ventured to square this generally accepted thought with the notion of a 'God that had created the Universe'.

In relation to this question, various different philosophical viewpoints of how reality actually functions have been developed. These bridge both questions concerning the nature of human consciousness as well as external physical reality and the interaction between them. The different standpoints reflect where the alternate schools of thought believe the focus of reality lies.

These can be briefly summarized as below:

o Solipsism – The view or theory that the self is all that can be known to exist.

- Idealism – Things exist only as ideas in the mind rather than as material objects independent of the mind.

- Realism – The theory that physical objects continue to exist whether they are perceived or not.

- Naïve Realism – The doctrine that in perception of physical objects what is before the mind is the object itself and not a representation of it.

- Materialism – The philosophic doctrine that matter is the only reality and that everything in the world, including thought, will and feeling, can be explained in terms of matter alone.

o   Naturalism – An ideological account of the world in terms of the causes and natural forces that rejects all spiritual, supernatural or teleological explanations. This is often taken to run in parallel to the methodology of science.

o   Theism – The belief in the existence of a God or gods.

o   Atheism – The belief that there is no God or gods, or denial that God or gods exist.

Other concepts of interest include:

o Anthropic Principle – a philosophical consideration that observations of the Universe must be compatible with the conscious and sapient life that observes it.

o Monism – the doctrine that the person consists of only a single substance, or that there is no crucial difference between mental and physical events or properties.

o Dualism (mind–body) – the view of mind that mental phenomena are, in some respects, non-physical, or that the mind and body are distinct and separable.

Prior to the era of modern physics, in the 18th/19th centuries the doctrine of 'philosophical naturalism' had over time become the dominant view of reality and nature. Since then, science and naturalism have been largely argued to 'walk hand-in-hand' with any notion of 'supernatural' or 'deliberate cause' being long consigned to history as at best metaphysics or often simply regarded as pure irrational nonsense. The Universe was still generally believed at this time to be eternal and therefore a naturalistic explanation for the origin of nature was not even required. This thinking went on to solidify a typically realistic/materialistic and ultimately atheistic outlook of the Universe.

This scientific approach since the Renaissance has been extraordinarily successful and the whole of the modern technological revolution that has occurred since has arisen entirely from this discipline. However, for science itself now to make discoveries that potentially challenge the naturalist 'mindset' would come arguably as quite a revelation to the vast majority of people who have ever studied science (including the author). It is fair to say that many would not have predicated this as the outcome that was expected after roughly 400 years of modern scientific enquiry.

However, in the early 20th century came the astounding experimental discovery made by Edwin Hubble (published 1929 with a value of the Hubble constant) that the Universe was actually expanding. It's less known that this idea was, in fact, derived theoretically earlier by Alexander Friedmann (published 1922) using the theory of General Relativity. This result, of course, ran contrary to all the thinking of that time and centuries before. Ironically, in response this discovery, Einstein then introduced the 'Cosmological Constant' as essentially a fudge factor into the General Relativity field equation in order to overcome this problem. This Cosmological Constant has since become one of the cornerstones of the key arguments to be discussed later in the book. The concept known as the 'Hubble flow' demonstrates that galaxies obey a simple rule that the further they are away the proportionately faster they are receding (their radial speed). This can be seen in the diagram below plotting their speed against their distance from the Earth:

Diagram of the 'Hubble flow' of galaxies:

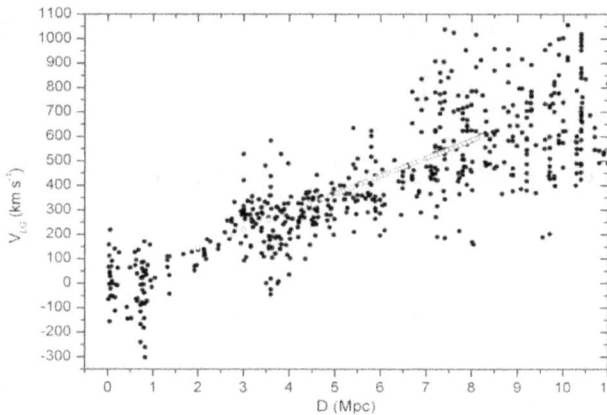

This discovery led to the certain conclusion that the Universe indeed had a definite temporal beginning and had *not* always existed – famously mocked by the astronomer Fred Hoyle as the 'Big Bang' (although the name stuck). The problem of the conundrum of the origin of Universe had now become central to the question of the scientific study of the Universe, with all the philosophical and logical problems that come with it. This discovery, along with the massive developments in pure physics over the course of that century and into the 21st century, has actually created a picture of nature which is now generally incompatible with the commonly held notions of naturalism.

The following discussion seeks to outline the debatable current status of naturalist and realist views in relation to the origin of the Universe. This is based entirely upon evidence, scientific data and inexorable physical theory which demonstrates that modern physics and cosmology really leave only two subsequent possible rational positions to hold: theism or solipsism. There is in reality found to be little place for realism, materialism and hence naturalism/atheism in modern physics and cosmology. Those notions underpinned by the naturalist worldview pertaining that the 'material world is all that exists', are in fact found to be experimentally refuted.

As mentioned in the introduction, the modern scientific debate concerning the origin of the Universe arguably now hinges against two distinct areas of physics and cosmology which have come to be appreciated over the course of the last century. These include the concept known as the Fine-Tuning Problem (FTP), which essentially bridges fundamental physics, particle physics and cosmology; and quantum mechanics, in particular the problem known as the Quantum Measurement Problem (QMP).

3. The Mathematical basis of the laws of nature

Pythagoras:

"...all things are number...

...God built the Universe on numbers..."

In the discussion of the FTP problem (focus of the next chapter) it is informative to clearly discuss what's actually being 'finely-tuned' in the first place. Many readers, who are not particularly interested in mathematics, could arguably pass over this chapter if they wished onto the next. But it is instructive to discuss the background of these critical quantities that are in question.

In the broadest sense any mathematical relationship relates variable quantities between each other; any constant terms are either innately measured values or proportionality values which dictate the strength and scale of the interaction in question.

To summarize, there are arguably two distinct types of 'constant quantities' found in physics:

1. Quantities describing a fixed innate property of a given object (i.e. the charge of an electron).

2. Constants of proportionality arising between the relationships of the variable terms within an equation. These are typically interpreted

physically, as representing the strength of the described interaction (i.e. Newton's gravitational constant).

It is the precisely the strength and scale of these constant quantities found in the mathematical 'laws of nature' that the FTP is concerned with, not the actual form of these relationships (laws) in themselves. The FTP does not in any way modify the laws of nature, whose origins are equally independently entirely a mystery. But precisely dictates the strength and scale of their interactions. This is what profoundly governs the allowed structure and evolution of what's observed in the Universe, both in form and on all length-scales. Whether the laws of nature themselves were equally invented at the moment of the Big Bang or existed 'prior' to it, is another question entirely.

Experimental research is, of course, the source of all 'real-world' data, which provides the assessment and cornerstone of all knowledge of the natural world. In terms of describing natural processes, the discipline of theoretical physics is essentially an exercise in applied mathematics. The laws of nature are indeed described entirely mathematically. This notion is by no means a modern idea; back in ancient times this insight was already very much in place. Perhaps most famously popularized by the Greek philosopher Pythagoras (who lived roughly 6th century BC) under the view that '*all things are number*'. Although it should be noted in modern physics this involves much more than mere arithmetic, advanced calculus and geometry being the cornerstone of most physical theories.

Fundamentally, most quantities in nature generally seem to be related in terms of their multiplication or division, what's commonly known in mathematics as either direct or inverse proportion (which has the mathematical symbol $\propto$. Also, many natural interactions follow what are known as power relationships, being proportionate to a power of a given quantity, i.e. a square or a cube such as in the famous equation: $E = mc^2$.

Usually physical laws are typically of some variance of the following formats:

Direct proportion:

$QuantityA \propto QuantityB \times QuantityC$

Inverse proportion: $Quantity\ A \propto \dfrac{QuantityB}{QuantityC}$

Power relations: $QuantityA \propto QuantityB^2$

More complex relationships often involve the branch of mathematics which deals with the behavior of nonlinear variables known as calculus (mentioned earlier). This results in most laws involving either multiplication or division operations rather an addition and subtraction. Perhaps this is one of the reasons Renaissance scientists greatly preferred Arabic numerals over Roman numerals, given the former are much easier to use in terms of multiplication and division but not necessarily in terms of addition and subtraction.

Another odd observation is in just how many different branches/categories of such knowledge in both mathematics and the physical sciences are typically grouped into sets of three distinct laws, rules or statements (examples are listed at the end of the chapter). By no means is this a universal finding and whether this is likely entirely a coincidence is unclear, and the discussion is of a rather metaphysical nature. However, it could be pointed out that there are fundamentally three spatial dimensions alongside the 4th dimension of time in the Universe. This yields three 'degrees of freedom' in nature in which things can move but there is no such freedom in the flow of time (time always ticks forward). Could the common ordering of the laws of mathematics and nature into groups of typically 'triplet laws or statements' be a partial consequence of these three degrees of freedom found in nature? More interestingly, no law of physics bar one suggests that time should be fixed flowing forward and not backward (i.e. without a degree of freedom). The single exception to this is an area of physics known as thermodynamics, which in fact comprises four fundamental laws. Although it should be noted the additional so-called '0th law' was introduced into thermodynamics as late as 1935 (thus resulting in the total of four laws in that case). The only known physical law which suggests time must flow in one direction is, in fact, the 2nd law of thermodynamics. Interesting then, is it not, that thermodynamics has four known laws rather than the often typical three, possibly reflecting the influence of four factors/freedoms over three? Although this law, of course, explains the lack of a degree freedom in the time dimension. It is as though an additional law has been added alongside the usual customary three, like a joker added to a pack of cards. Many would certainly agree the 2nd law of thermodynamics holds a special place in physics, although it has also been suggested the 2nd law could be actually split into two pieces.

While it could be seen as an entirely metaphysical speculation, could this be taken as a philosophical argument against additional spatial dimensions in nature? These have been often speculated about in certain areas of modern physics, largely from theories such as supergravity and superstrings. Evidence for them, however, has been very hard to find.

Some examples of the various distinct physical categories, relationships and subject areas which commonly hold to 'triplet' laws in the form of postulates, states, forms or concepts: (NB: Note out of interest how none of them are rooted in biology.)

3 Components of space (The Spatial triplet):

(1) Height

(2) Width

(3) Depth

3 Components of time (The Temporal triplet):

(1) Past

(2) Present

(3) Future

3 Components of matter (The Material triplet):

(1) Solid

(2) Liquid

(3) Gas

NB: Plasma is not a '4th state of matter', but simply high energy ionized gas (no transitional phase involved).

3 Statements of basic logic (Aristotle, et al):

(1) The law of identity – "Whatever is, is". $A = A$

(2) The law of non-contradiction – "Two or more contradictory statements cannot both be true in the same sense at the same time".

(i.e. The statements $A=B$ and $A \neq B$ are mutually exclusive.)

(3) The law of excluded middle – "Everything must either be or not be, for every proposition either its positive or negative form is true". $A \neq \acute{A}$

3 Forms/types of probability:

(1) 'Geometrical' probabilities based on physical symmetries

(2) 'Empirical' probabilities based on prior data/results

(3) 'Judgmental' probabilities based on prior decisions

3 Laws of linear motion (Newton):

(1) Every object moves in a straight line unless acted upon by a force.

(2) The acceleration of an object is directly proportional to the net force exerted and inversely proportional to the object's mass.

$(F = ma)$

(3) For every action, there is an equal and opposite reaction.

[Out of interest, Newton's 3rd law is often identified as the technical analogy akin to the fundamental principles of Karma and the Daoist Yin/Yang balance found in eastern thought.]

3 Laws of angular motion (Newton):

(1) The rotational principle of inertia: In the absence of a net applied torque, the angular velocity remains unchanged.

(2) This is not as general a relationship as the linear one because the moment of inertia, I, is not strictly a scalar quantity. The rotational equation is limited to rotation about a single principal axis, which in simple cases is an axis of symmetry. ($\tau = I \alpha$)

(3) For every applied torque, there is an equal and opposite reaction torque. (Analogous to 3rd law of linear motion)

3 Laws of planetary motion (Johannes Kepler):

(1) The orbit of a planet is an ellipse with the Sun at one of the two foci.

(2) A line segment joining a planet and the Sun (at one focus) sweeps out equal areas during equal intervals of time.

(3) The square of the orbital period of a planet is proportional to the cube of the semi-major axis of its orbit.

3 Point definition of 'planetary status' (IAU):

(1) The body is the primary body of its system in orbit around its parent star.

(2) The body has sufficient mass to assume hydrostatic equilibrium. (Gravity is dominant enough to pull the object into a spherical shape, then consequently adjusted by its intrinsic rotation, i.e. 'oblation'.)

(3) The body has 'cleared its neighborhood' around its orbit by absorbing or displacing any neighboring debris – failure of this particular criterion relegates the body to 'dwarf planet' status.

3 Distinct underlying basic principles of Quantum Mechanics:

Briefly summarized:

(1) Wave particle duality (Erwin Schrödinger, et al)

(2) The uncertainty principle (Heisenberg)

$$\Delta p . \Delta x \geq \frac{\hbar}{2}$$

(3) The exclusion principle (Pauli)

3 Main categories of Chemistry:

(1) Physical Chemistry

(2) Organic Chemistry

(3) Inorganic Chemistry

3 Fundamental laws of Chemistry (Dalton et al):

(1) Law of Mass Conservation: Matter is neither created nor destroyed in ordinary chemical reactions.

(2) Law of Definite Proportions: Different samples of a pure compound always contain the same proportions of elements by mass.

(3) Law of Multiple Proportions: Elements can combine in different ways to form different chemical compounds, with mass ratios that are small whole-number multiples of each other.

3 Laws of Reflection (Ptolemy, Ibn Sahl, et al):

(1) The incident ray, the reflected ray and the normal to the reflection surface at the point of the incidence lie in the same plane.

(2) The angle which the incident ray makes with the normal is equal to the angle which the reflected ray makes to the same normal.

(3) The reflected ray and the incident ray are on the opposite sides of the normal.

3 Laws of Electrostatics (Coulomb, et al):

(1) The force is directly proportional to the product of their strengths.

(2) The force is inversely proportional to the square of the distance between them.

(3) The force is inversely proportional to the absolute permittivity of the surrounding medium. This is known as Coulomb's Law.

The 3 Laws of Magnetism (Gilbert, Faraday, et al):

(1) Energy is required to create a magnet, but no energy is required to maintain a magnet (magnetic field).

(2) Like poles repel each other, and unlike poles attract each other.

(3) The magnetic force between two poles is directly proportional to the pole strength and inversely proportional to the square of the distance between them.

3 Types of Black Holes (Schwarzschild, Hawkings, et al):

(1) Primordial black hole – formed at the beginning of the Universe from the remnants of the Big Bang singularity

(2) Stellar origin black hole – formed from the supernova pressure of a large dying star acting to collapse its core

(3) Supermassive black hole – formed as the gravitational heart of a galaxy's center

3 'Laws' of Robotics (Isaac Asimov):

Though obviously rooted in fiction, many would argue they actually hold some credence in the now emerging realm of AI:

(1) A robot may not injure a human being or, through inaction, allow a human being to come to harm.

(2) A robot must obey the orders given it by human beings except where such orders would conflict with the First Law.

(3) A robot must protect its own existence as long as such protection does not conflict with the First or Second Laws.

Finally:

4 Laws of thermodynamics (Carnot, Clausius, et al):

Interestingly, the classical theory of thermodynamics actually is described to pertain to 4 distinct laws (though some even say 5, also proposing an even more fundamental underlying '-1th law' of thermodynamics as a deeper explanation).

Note the 2nd Law is arguably the only known concept in physics that actually suggests the very familiar concept of the 'arrow of time' – time always flowing forwards in one direction, never backwards.

(1) 0th law: If two systems are in thermal equilibrium with a third system, they are in thermal equilibrium with each other. This law helps define the concept of temperature.

(2) 1st law: When energy passes, as work, as heat, or with matter, into or out from a system, the system's internal energy changes in accord with the law of conservation of energy. Equivalently, perpetual motion machines of the first kind (machines that produce work with no energy input) are impossible.

(3) 2nd Law: In a natural thermodynamic process, the sum of the entropies of the interacting thermodynamic systems always increases.

Equivalently, perpetual motion machines of the second kind (machines that spontaneously convert thermal energy into mechanical work) are impossible.

(4) 3rd Law: The entropy of a system approaches a constant value as the temperature approaches absolute zero. With the exception of non-crystalline solids (glasses) the entropy of a system at absolute zero is typically close to zero and is equal to the natural logarithm of the product of the quantum ground states.

4. The Fine-Tuning Problem (FTP)

Fred Hoyle:

"...a commonsense interpretation of the facts suggests that a superintellect has monkeyed with physics, as well as with chemistry and biology, and that there are no blind forces worth speaking about in nature. The numbers one calculates from the facts seem to me so overwhelming as to put this conclusion almost beyond question..."

In the realm of physics there are many quantities known as the 'fundamental constants'. These are fixed values measured experimentally that define the strength and behavior of physical interactions and/or the properties of fundamental forces and particles. The laws of physics do NOT explain the values of the fundamental constants, they simply use them.

The FTP is not a specific physical theory as such but essentially an underlying realization that the formation of the Universe as we observe it, that allows complicated structure to exist on all length scales, is poised on an incredible knife-edge balance. This, amongst other things, allows for the unlikely existence of biological life which ultimately relies on the balancing of the physical constants to an enormous degree.

There are many examples of the FTP in action in nature (see Appendix 1). However, several of these require values that are accurate to such an enormous degree that any notion put forward that this phenomenon is merely an 'uncaused coincidence' can only be described as utterly absurd and irrational. A good example of this is the fusing of hydrogen nuclei into helium, the primary energy releasing process in stars such as the Sun. The amount of matter converted by this process is 0.7%; if the value deviated even slightly to, say, 0.6%, the proton would be unable to combine with the neutron to create helium. The entire Universe would therefore consist of only hydrogen gas – higher elements, chemistry, rocky planets and of course biological life, would be impossible. Conversely, if the value was only slightly higher, say 0.8%, hydrogen would be fused away at such a prestigious rate such that almost all of it would have been 'burned away' in the Big Bang, long before any stars had formed. The previous example, in fact, is a relatively mild example of FTP in terms of the maximum deviation, but the level of being conveniently 'just right' is apparent again and again in nature. Some of the more extreme examples are listed in the following table in which the level of maximum deviation is incredibly sensitive:

Fine-tuning of the physical forces/constants of the Universe:

Parameter	Max. deviation permissible
Ratio of Electrons/Protons	1 part in 10^{37}
Ratio of the Electromagnetic Force/Gravity	1 part in 10^{40}
Expansion Rate of Universe	1 part in 10^{55}
Mass Density of Universe	1 part in 10^{59}
Cosmological Constant	1 part in 10^{120}

(For a broader more detailed list, see also Appendix 1.)

Perhaps the most extreme example of fine-tuning comes from the relatively recent experimental confirmation of the Cosmological Constant. Not only was its existence being confirmed a surprise (Saul Perlmutter, et al. 1998), but its actual behaviour was equally very unexpected. The Universe is, in fact, expanding at an ever-increasing rate; to put it another way, the Hubble flow is, in fact, actually accelerating. The discovery was very much the reverse to the widely assumed result that the expansion would be slowing due to gravitational breaking. However, far more unsettling was the level of fine-tuning required for this constant, setting the arguable current 'record' that any deviation from 1 part in 10^{120} the Universe would either accelerate so rapidly that no stars could ever form or rapidly collapse in the converse. To elucidate a number of that magnitude, consider there are an estimated 10^{19} number of sand grains on all the beaches and deserts upon the surface of the whole Earth – the Cosmological Constant's fine-tuning is a 100 orders of magnitude larger than that number.

Does that figure sound consistent with the suggestion that the Universe's structure is a mere 'accident of nature'?

How many sand grains exist on all the combined beaches and deserts upon the Earth's surface today?

The sheer number and level of cross dependency of these finely tuned constants make the clear case that the Universe at its origin was indeed intelligently designed at the cosmological level at least. Which leads to the unavoidable subsequent conclusion that an intelligently designed Universe has to be the result of an intelligent designer. It is hard to perceive of how this could ever be explained in terms of any naturalistic/uncaused Universe consisting of only material reality. There is simply no way to explain the level of fine-tuning by simple natural random processes. This represents clear teleological influence on the nature at its most fundamental level. This is certainly no 'God of the gaps' argument; these results affect every single particle, entity, structure and interaction at any level and length scale contained within the Universe. Both in terms of their behavior and existence.

The common counterargument to this notion is the postulate that our Universe is simply one existing in a wider 'multiverse' structure and the fine tuning is an inevitable fluke amongst these countless billions and billions of 'other universes'. A sort of vain appeal to a reversed anthropic principle. In reality, there is no theoretical basis for the 'multiverse' concept to exist and not a shred of experimental data to support it. However, there seems to be a great hankering after this 'multiverse' notion within the academic realm precisely because of an ideological desire to find a strong denial of the clear implications of the FTP problem. (This will be discussed in more detail later in the book.) Indeed, we see regular research articles in the popular media extoling the important matter of the 'multiverse and separate universes' as though this was the most pressing question in modern science. The urgency of finding parallel universes separate from our own is about as pressing as finding fairies at the bottom of the garden. There is truly no great rush in researching these 'other universes', because the study of unnecessary and speculative metaphysical notions is really not that important. In actuality our knowledge of this Universe remains in its infancy. Indeed, physics cannot even fully explain the motion of a bicycle. Dealing with the endless unexplained phenomena of this the real measurable Universe should be the focus of true science.

So why then is there such a great ideological rush to debunk the FTP? Why not immediately also debunk the 'multiverse' concept at the same time, which has no evidential basis in the first place? Is it because the evidence-based ramifications of the FTP are unpalatable to the academic elite? The reality is this: the left-wing academics that populate the ivory towers of most universities are rattled, because they are only too well aware that real physics (that's actually based on evidence and has survived endless falsification testing) is clearly pushing headlong into the opposite direction of their secular/atheistic political slant and points entirely to a theistic basis of this, the one real observed Universe. The observed FTP phenomenon undeniably represents God's fingerprints on the natural world.

5. The Quantum Measurement Problem (QMP)

Eugene Wigner:

"...while Solipsism may be logically consistent with present Quantum Mechanics, Monism in the sense of Materialism is not..."

The revolutionary advent of quantum mechanics in the early part of the 20th century turned science on its head. Gone were the certain predictable systems or the prosaic 'clockwork universe' of Sir Isaac Newton; instead a world of probabilities and uncertainty ruled. But to a greater extent, it returned science back to fundamental questions which had long been sidelined into the realm of philosophy for many centuries. These questions focus on whether the Universe is really based on an external material reality. Does the Universe and the many constituents that it contains exist independently of human thought?

For many today and historically this question may seem quite odd; most would assume the 'realism' of the world, and of those, many would equally hold to the more extreme version of realism (materialism) that postulates that all that exists is simply particles of matter and radiation and their common interaction.

This debate has flowed for many centuries, nonetheless, from the classical world harkening back to the great academic debate between Plato (idealism) and Aristotle (realism/materialism).

Aristotle argued towards an independent reality entirely unconnected to human thought; observed reality defines what is independently actually true/extant and therefore it defines the best it can ever be. This notion has largely become the predominant view of reality. Plato conversely argued for an 'idealistic' view of the Universe in which there exist fundamental 'ideal forms', but the observed objects of the worlds that we perceive are simply imperfect imitations of these 'ideal forms'. Primarily that the 'perfect conceptual form' exists in our minds initially and we then attach these 'ideal forms' onto the objects we perceive in the world; therefore particular concepts can only exist because 'ideal universal forms' exist in the first place. Plato famously discussed the 'allegory of the cave' conjecture in which 'all knowledge' can only be held as a mere shadow of reality and truth.

Unfortunately quantum mechanics brings such esoteric debate back into the centre of scientific discussion (from the understanding known as the 'Copenhagen interpretation'). The question of whether material reality is independent of thought has returned and cannot be avoided.

The famous Young's slit experiment (diagram below) demonstrates the fundamental question of quantum mechanics and leads to the QMP issue. By firing a coherent beam through two slits and recording the resultant pattern created on the screen, this experiment elucidated the idea of 'wave–particle' duality. Which may at first sound innocent but leads to endless problems with the concept if reality, precisely because it applies equally to not only massless–radiation particles (e.g. photons) but also to material particles (e.g. electrons).

Diagram of the famous 'Young's slit' experiment:

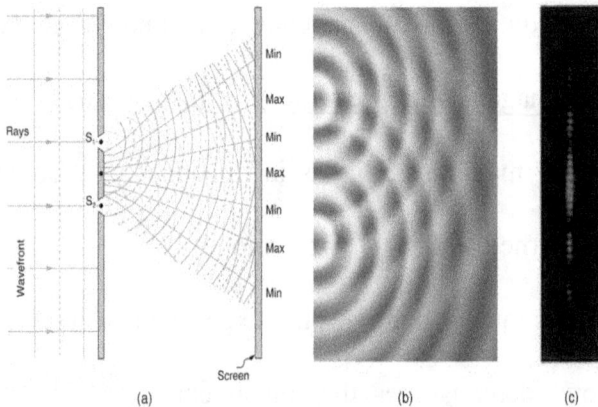

(a)   (b)   (c)

The act of observation appears to fundamentally alter the observed state of the particle in question. When no attempt to measure what is occurring within the slits is made, a standard wave–like interference pattern is always observed. The moment any attempt is made to discern the 'actual path' of any particular particle by placing an observation device either side of the slits the expected particle form is seen. The conclusion of these experiments (after many years of deliberation) demonstrates that observation alters reality itself and observation alone is what forces anything to become a specific form – it could be interpreted that nature is indeed fundamentally 'idealistic' as Plato described, contrary to what most people think.

'Material reality', a notion that the Universe exists outside conscious observation is experimentally falsified by the results of these experiments and many others.

Many scientists initially, no less than the calibre of people such as Albert Einstein, De Broglie and Schrödinger, seriously disliked the clear if disturbing ramifications of quantum mechanics, and introduced additional concepts into the theory (so-called 'hidden-variable' theories) in an attempt to recover an underlying classical/material reality. In the 1980s an idea formulated by the physicist John Steward Bell was put to the test, known as the Bell inequality. This aimed to produce a clear experimental test as to whether the act of observation truly decides reality or whether an underlying material reality exists independent of observation (i.e. debunk 'hidden-variable' theories). The experimental results (Alan Aspect et al, 1982) unequivocally state that the former is correct, observation alone decides what is real – there is no material reality independent of observation. Another interesting conclusion to be drawn from this experiment involves the behavior of particles which are linked together in a relationship known as a 'quantum entangled state'. This demonstrates that the information exchanged between entangled particles does indeed travel instantaneously (i.e. infinite speed) between them, whereas in contrast, as we know from the theory of special relativity (Albert Einstein, 1905), matter cannot travel faster than light. This suggests information cannot therefore be material in nature, but also is arguably more fundamental than matter as the dominant influence.

More recently, increasingly detailed experiments have been conducted to test these results further. The results of experiments known as 'delayed choice quantum eraser' (DCQE) experiments (from 1999) have further solidified these notions (diagram below). These experiments are highly intriguing as they further increase the difficulty of separating

conscious observation from the results.

Diagram of a 'Delayed choice quantum eraser' experiment:

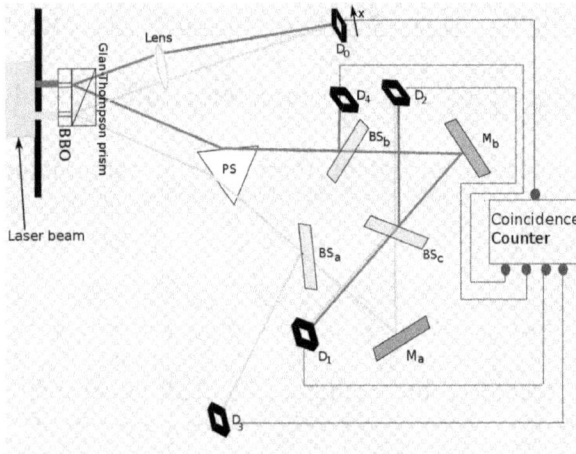

Here the detector is placed beyond the exit side of

the Young's slits and pulled backwards when the

beam passes through. If the wave form was still

observed, the beam would go through the slits as a

wave and the presence of an observer would not

fundamentally alter the nature of the beam. Surprisingly, the opposite is observed, and a particle form is what is actually observed. This means that not only does the mere presence of an observer force the beam into a particle form at later measurement, but even more strangely its very presence causes a 'new history to be back uploaded' in the first place. Literally interpreted, history itself is altered by the presence of an observer – only the currently 'confirmed history' in the present moment is actually valid. This turns reality/causality on its head; normally it thought the present moment must be constrained by what occurred in the past – in fact the past appears altered to be consistent with the observed present (retro-causality).

The ancient eastern philosophers had always said that the past and future do not exist, only the present moment matters and indeed is what actually can be even said to exist. The conscious thoughts in the present moment decide what is actually real/occurring in the moment – the 'mind alone creates reality'. Thousands of years later, modern quantum mechanics appears to closely concur with this view of the reality. Additionally, more recent experiments undertaken since further consolidate this view, concepts known as the Kochen-Specker theorem and Leggett's inequality have been experimentally confirmed, further debunking counter-concepts such as naïve realism.

Material reality *'does not exist'* as Wigner originally stated; for anything to exist it must be at first observed in order to 'lock it down' into existence. Albert Einstein once remarked in relation to quantum mechanics *'...does the Moon then not exist unless I'm looking at it...?'* – Surprisingly the answer to that question (and any of similar form) appears to be very much 'yes'. Indeed, how do you or I even know that we exist? Do we all also require an external observer to 'lock us into existence' or do we do that within our own self-consciousness? Here the debate between the two 'scientifically consistent' notions, theism and the logically more extreme view solipsism now fully arises.

Ultimately (as the argument goes), the only consistent conclusion leads inexorably into a logical regression that demands that there has to exist a default 'cosmological observer'. This 'cosmological observer' has to exist in order to 'lock' the Universe into a state of being in the first place. This problem occurs always in the present moment of observation/experience – the present moment being the only thing that it can be sure truly exists. The argument therefore concludes that without an all-encompassing 'omniscient observer' at the cosmological level, the Universe simply could not exist at all in any sense that we understand it. Ultimately, that unless you believe in solipsism – God has to exist. This conclusion has nothing to do with metaphysics or religion but is an inexorable consequence of the experimental results of quantum mechanics.

6. The Counterarguments to FTP and QMP

G.K. Chesterton:

"...when people stop believing in God, they don't believe in nothing... they believe in everything..."

The following section details and outlines many of the common counterarguments put forward against the concepts and conclusions put forward in the previously discussed chapters. These generally describe arguments against those implying a theistic basis of the origin of the Universe, with a subsequent recourse against each of them in turn.

6.1 The 'Multiverse' concept – a counter argument to FTP

Steven Weinberg:

"...I don't think one should underestimate the fix we're in, that in the end we will not be able to explain the world, that we will have some laws (or some set of laws) of nature that we are not be able to derive them on the grounds simply of mathematical consistency – because we can already think of mathematically consistent laws that don't describe the world as we know it... and we will

always be left with a question – why are the laws of nature what they are rather than some other laws..."

The FTP concept is in many ways the modern form of the 'teleological argument', as championed by many philosophers and theologians over the ages (e.g. Al-Ghazali, St. Thomas Aquinas, Averroes (Ibn Rashd), William Paley, etc.). This concept states that nature is full of examples of empirical design. However (the teleological argument), in its modern form, the FTP poses a serious challenge to any purely naturalist/materialist interpretation of reality.

There are arguably few serious counterarguments that have been put forward against FTP, but the most common is known as the 'Multiverse' concept. Put simply, this is an idea that many separate/independent universes have formed which hold different fundamental physical laws and constants and therefore a life/human-friendly universe(s) was inevitable because of the sheer number of possibilities.

It is initially very important to clarify a major misconception that often arises in relation to the 'Multiverse' concept which can often be seen in popular discussion and forums. There are two very similar sounding concepts in modern physics which are in fact completely different phenomena. These are:

1. The 'many-worlds' interpretation of quantum physics

2. The 'Multiverse' theory

The first is an interpretation of how quantum physics actually manifests in the physical world and is held in contrast to the Copenhagen interpretation; this notion was originally put forward by Hugh Everett (1957). Although in basic terms it does describe parallel worlds existing together in a common phase space, this description pertains entirely to our own specific Universe and its specific laws. If it is the correct description of nature, this is simply how our own single Universe works, and has nothing to do with other universes (i.e. the 'Multiverse').

The second concept is the one which is commonly held (amongst other things) as a rebuttal of the FTP. This is the notion that there exists an infinite number of distinct physical universes that are separate to each other, have separate origins and their own distinct physical laws and potentially even different numbers of spatial dimensions.

Although currently a source of great discussion and debate it must be emphasized that the 'Multiverse' has no real supporting evidence whatsoever, and furthermore, it has no theoretical basis on any established physical theory either. It can only be described as pure speculation and even at the most simple level it can immediately be criticized on basic philosophical grounds, such as Occam's razer (the Law of Parsimony) – a principle according to which *an explanation of a thing or event is made with the fewest possible assumptions'*.

Inventing an infinite number of 'parallel universes' with different physical laws in order to 'explain away' the FTP (essentially because the implications of FTP are seen as unpalatable) is an incredibly weak argument. The 'Multiverse' concept is pure unsupported conjecture which is in strong contrast to the mountain of detailed experimental data and robust theoretical support that underpins the physics that leads to the FTP.

6.2 The theistic creation dilemma: 'if God created the Universe, then who in turn created God?'

Richard Dawkins:

"...theists say God did it – that of course is no explanation at all, because it leaves unexplained the tuner. It just pushes the problem back one step..."

A common argument involves the notion that if a 'creator' created the Universe, then who in turn created the 'creator'? This therefore results in a logical infinite regression loop. Every creation would also in turn need a creator – ad infinitum. This is a common argument that has also been used historically in a reversed form in order to argue in favour of theism, a typical example being from St. Thomas Aquinas's 'four cosmological arguments', i.e. the 'unmoved mover', the 'uncaused causer', etc. The implied infinite regression is therefore taken as a positive argument for God to exist precisely to break the infinite loop.

This in the modern context has been arguably superseded and fails to recognize the 'source and effect' relationship that underpins much of physics. Just as the subject and the object are fundamentally distinct and cannot be each other, the apparent cannot be the source. As is often said, you cannot get drunk on the word 'wine'; you have to drink it.

To give an example, this is like stating: James Clerk Maxwell's theory of electromagnetism has 'no value because we cannot explain the prior nature of electric charge'. We know electric charge exists because it is required – because electromagnetism is well observed, and its effects are well understood theoretically and experimentally.

By the same logic:

1. The FTP implies a 'fine-tuner'.

2. The QMP implies a 'cosmological observer/ measurer'.

Does the fact we have no real conception of the prior nature of electric charge mean a theory of electromagnetism that suggests the existence of the electric charge is *'no explanation at all, that it just pushes it back one step'*? A rather flawed argument, logically and scientifically. Most of science is based on concepts of quantities whose fundamental nature is entirely undetermined, but their effects are well measured and understood – primary examples:

Source   **Resultant Effect**

Electric Charge	Electromagnetism
Color Charge	Strong Nuclear Force
Mass/Energy	Gravity
Inertia (mass)	Resistance to accelerated motion

There is a strong logical and physical distinction between the driving source (whose underlying nature is often obscure) and its resultant effects (usually well observed and understood mathematically).

You do not reject electromagnetism because you cannot explain what electric charge is. You do not reject gravity because you cannot explain what mass/energy is. Again, you do not reject the strong nuclear force because you cannot explain what color charge is. Therefore, do you reject the fine-tuning problem because you cannot explain what the 'fine-tuner' is? Equally, do you reject the consequences of the quantum mechanics, because you cannot explain the nature of the inferred 'cosmological-observer'?

The argument put forward at the beginning of this section would be to largely challenge the underlying understanding of much of fundamental physics. The prior nature of the 'fine tuner/cosmological observer' as required by the FTP and QMP problems is not understood in the same fashion, but its requirement to exist is palpable. The fact that you cannot explain or understand its prior 'nature or form' is totally irrelevant. In fact, it is precisely the obscurity of these 'fundamental sources' that gives them their power. If they were easily dissectible, they would lose much of their all-encompassing and explanative authority. From the intangible you may just glimpse the truly fundamental. As is beautifully reflected in the first verse of the two-and-a-half-thousand- year-old Chinese philosophical tome the Dao De Jing:

The Dao that can be told, is not the eternal Dao.

The name that can be named, is not the eternal

name.

The Dao is both named and nameless

As nameless it is the origin of all things,

as named it is the Mother of 10,000 things.

The flow of time is always forward. This implies the 'source' always begets the 'effect', never the other way round. The argument of infinite regression (as alluded to at the start of this chapter) is incorrectly treating this flow in reverse, creating a false paradox. The observed effect always implies the source; the source is already extant by definition. The logical deduction of its existence then immediately manifests itself by consequence of its observation. Just as you cannot get rain without a cloud, or a warm sunny day without the sun shining, let alone electromagnetic effects without the existence of the mysterious concept of electric charge, etc. Likewise, the FTP concept demands by observational fact the existence of a 'fine-tuner' and likewise the QMP implies the requirement of a default 'cosmological observer/measurer'. Ultimately, observational fact totally supersedes any erstwhile purely logical argument and speculation.

For those who might wish to downplay such an analogy, consider: what is the actual basis of physics? Essentially physics describes the allowed path of any given object whilst being constrained by the natural external forces acting upon it. Take, for example, the now commonly popularized 'Standard

Model' of physics, these days often seen to be printed on t-shirts for discussion and amusement.

As with many such modern theories of physics, the primary quantity known as the Lagrangian (symbol L) is usually set in equality to many effective terms on the right-hand side of the equation. The Lagrangian quantity, in fact, precisely describes in mathematical terms the allowed path of a given object in relation to its current applied circumstances. That circumstance (or environment) would entail the given forces, fields, etc. it is currently exposed to.

The 'Standard Model' of physics in a popular shorthand form:

$$\mathcal{L} = -\frac{1}{4} F_{\mu v} F^{\mu v}$$

$$+ i \bar{\psi} \mathcal{D} \psi + h \cdot c$$

$$+ \bar{\psi}_i y_{ij} \psi_i \phi + h \cdot c$$

$$+ \left| \mathcal{D}_\mu \phi \right|^2 - V(\phi)$$

Is the Lagrangian not, in fact, arguably a technical description that could be set in analogy to the traditional/poetic concept of the Dao? The term 'Dao' roughly translates into English as the 'path' or the 'way'. The analogy between physics and Daoism has been made before; indeed, both revolve around the fundamental question of the path anything might/should take with emphasis on the present moment. By implication, perhaps those ancient thinkers had access to similar wisdom that experimental physics has today uncovered, that the more obscure the concept of the underlying source the more descriptive power the concept holds. The obscurity is a good thing, not a bad thing.

6.3 The 'intelligence must emerge late' concept

Carl G. Jung

"...People will do anything, no matter how absurd, in order to avoid facing their own souls. One does not become enlightened by imagining figures of light, but by making the darkness conscious..."

Another common naturalist/atheist notion argues that advanced intelligence could not have been present at the origin of the Universe because such a complex property 'must arrive late on'.

This is a good example of an argument which assumes a great deal a priori; it assumes all things obey the classical flow of time and that the concept of intelligence exists in purely biological terms. These assumptions are arguably very flawed, particularly in view of much of modern scientific understanding. In physics we now appear to face the necessity of a much broader and immaterial notion of consciousness and intelligent observation (ultimately leading to the logical inevitability for the need of the existence of a 'cosmological observer' as required by the QMP). This clearly lies outside the realm of pure biology. But this argument also places no recognition of the inexorable experimental data implying 'intelligent input' at the origin of the Universe (as required by the FTP). This very biocentric view of all notions of consciousness /intelligence that might exist is clearly incompatible with those aforementioned ideas. Equally it also erroneously assumes that all things have to develop along the 'classical worldline' understanding of time in order to make the conclusion that 'intelligence must arrive late'. The 'cosmological observer' sits outside the flow of time and is present in all moments; equally the fine-tuning had to be by definition undertaken at the moment of the Big Bang. The observational and experimental basis of these notions completely refutes the concept of 'late emergence'.

Does the lack of any strong scientific understanding of the nature of consciousness warrant the exclusive conflation of it as arising purely from biological minds? People who have testified to witnessing Poltergeist activity, for example, would certainly hold to the existence of the concept of disembodied consciousness and intelligence.

This biocentric view might be seen by many as a very rational viewpoint but what is the underlying scientific support for that strong viewpoint? The 'classical worldline' concept is completely invalidated by the known rules and experimental behavior of quantum mechanics. There is no fixed/defined past or future; only the eternal present defines reality. This, of course, is equally quite alien to classical Newtonian thought as it is to everyday human experience but is experimental fact. In this world something either definitely exists or it does not; in the certain sense of the eternal present moment such is the nature of the QMP.

In that context, there is no 'late on' or evolution in the biological sense for this fundamental consciousness. For the finely tuned Universe to exist in order to allow biological life to emerge, intelligence must have been present already to allow for such conditions to arise. Life is based on chemistry which in turn is fundamentally a quantum process (some even say the whole of chemistry is contained within the Schrödinger equation).

This a good example of a convincing but flawed argument, wrong not because it's an inconsistent argument, but because its key underlying premises are flawed. Being, the unfounded sole equivocation of consciousness/intelligence to biology and the presumption that all things develop against the flow of time in the classical sense.

6.4 Why not solipsism?

Bertrand Russell:

"...as against solipsism it is to be said, in the first place, that it is psychologically impossible to believe, and is rejected in fact even by those who mean to accept it. I once received a letter from an eminent logician, Mrs Christine Ladd-Franklin, saying that she was a solipsist, and was surprised that there were no others. Coming from a logician and a solipsist, her surprise surprised me..."

There's arguably no direct scientific evidence that can concretely dismiss solipsism. However, there are many philosophical arguments that can be put against it. The key aspect of solipsism is not simply a denial of material reality (which is frankly supported by experimental data) but the conceptual worldview that denies the existence of all other minds other than oneself. It is fair to remark (as aforementioned by Eugene Wigner) that one clear and valid interpretation of modern physics could indeed be taken as solipsistic. However, few can countenance it psychologically, but clearly that is a not in itself a hard disproof.

Solipsism would infer that all that exists is the product of the single mind of their self. Therefore, the immense complexities and functional structures seen in nature as well as the great achievements of many gifted human beings (such as the musical compositions of Beethoven, etc.), are all the product of the self. A rather unlikely prospect. Solipsism is effectively saying that the individual is essentially a 'god' unto themselves, again a rather odd viewpoint given the level of suffering they will inevitably experience. As Buddha pointed out that suffering is the result of the external world acting upon you against your conscious desires, the uncontrolled external world conflicting against your conscious will. Suffering (which is an inevitability to the individual self) makes little sense in terms of solipsism.

Contrary another major critic was Wittgenstein, who employed, for example, a quite different linguistic argument against it. Stating that solipsists communicate their ideas (to themselves or to others) using language. Language is a tool to communicate with other minds. By its nature, language derives its meaning from how other people use it. So a 'private language' (the only kind that can exist in solipsism) is by its nature meaningless. Therefore, any argument made by someone who is imagining the entire rest of the Universe is also meaningless, because it is necessarily made in a meaningless language.

The key argument against solipsism (taken in the context of the principal arguments contained in this book) must surely be the self-evident realization that our own personal human consciousness (that we are all equally self-aware of) is clearly not of the sufficient scale and scope that would be required to undertake the role of the 'fine-tuner/cosmological observer', etc. That, of course, is exactly what would be required in order for the Universe to be in the form and complexity that it appears to be; it is again self-evident to the individual that they are simply not up to the 'job description' of a creator. Can you design a Universe and affect a big bang? Can you alter and change the constants of nature? Can you turn amino acids into the inexplicable proteins of biology? Does your being exist outside the flow of time? In all these, I'd wager with some confidence the answer is a firm no and hence solipsism is an utter nonsense.

This is all valid unless you truly believe the world is just a 'pure figment' of your own imagination, then in that case everything and anything goes. Truly untestable and illogical.

6.5 The paradox of the quantum 'Universal locking problem'

Boëthius:

"...*God sees in the present the future events which proceed from apparent 'free choice'...*"

"...*Everything is known, not according to itself, but according to the capacity of the knower...*"

An important question into the nature of the quantum measurement problem (QMP) involves a paradoxical counterargument that could be made against the concept put forward previously in chapter 5. It could be cited that if the default 'cosmological observer observes all things' – then by consequence no subsequent 'quantum effects' could therefore ever be observed by anyone else in the first place (i.e. the universal locking problem).

The effect of an 'omniscient being observing the Universe' would surely be that any quantum probabilistic effects would be instantly collapsed into a specific state. Therefore, no human observer could subsequently ever perceive any observable quantum effects. These effects are, of course, well observed experimentally and the notion quantum mechanics arose precisely from such observations.

The apparent paradox is, therefore, we have the notion of the 'cosmological observer' as the inexorable conclusion arising from the QMP, but such a conclusion would in turn potentially diminish the very quantum observations that created the notion in the first place?

A possible answer to this very modern scientific conundrum could arguably be made from considering arguments put forward by an early medieval 6th century philosopher known as Boëthius. His argument develops unsurprisingly along the rather theological lines from that era but could be summarized as follows (this has been partially echoed by many other scholars in later times, such as St Augustine and John Calvin).

Boëthius – taking that the true initial premise of all wisdom is to be this:

'That God is the creator of all things, author and causer of all things, and alongside that equally it is understood that God exists only in the "eternal present" and is entirely outside the flow of time (that the observed natural world experiences). All things, therefore, are entirely known and entirely

predestined by God. God therefore knows both the past and the future, as well as the present, as we would think we know the present.'

Consequently, there is for us no real concept of free will – all things are completely predestined, in spite of all our innate instincts and predications to the contrary. Apparent free choice is not real free choice and by association, it could be argued that the concept of the 'cosmological observer' functions precisely as the 'great pre-destinator' of all things. This concept was earlier discussed by philosophers such as Aristotle, but his answer is not generally considered to be very clear. Boëthius's solution to this conundrum is that an event can be understood in different ways depending on the nature of the knower. Just as you could either choose to go shopping or take a walk in the park instead, predestined knowledge does not remove the apparent free choice of doing either activity; it simply demonstrates knowledge of the outcome that actually occurred (i.e. the 'truth-content' of the event). However, it could be argued that since the decision to either go shopping or walk in the park has yet to be made by the person, there isn't any real 'truth-content' that can be firmly attached to the event, and thus is it unknowable. Not even an omniscient entity can 'know the unknowable'. In any supposed prior decision, therefore, an important question of 'truth-content' should then be raised, and this is the critical point. In reality there is only the illusion of free will arising from an apparent 'transient or volatile will', in that the perceived prior decision points can sometimes, in fact, contain no real 'truth-content'.

It could be argued, if slightly circuitously, that localized Quantum events (such as observing the radioactive decay of an atom) are very much of a 'volatile unknowable nature' as described and hence their quantum uncertainty is very much observable in that instant. However, the events associated with larger macroscopic objects (such as the existence of the moon) are in contrast very much knowable, as their effects are not transient but widely affecting their environment. Hence quantum effects in the present moment can be observed by experimental scientists as there was no pre-existing 'truth-content' prior to their decision to make the transient and opportunist observation (and hence the subsequent events were not already 'locked down'). The rough limit of this effect appears to be around the level of the atomic scale; above this quantum effects are rarely seen; below this length scale they are the norm. This could suggest that this is the limit where objects arguably lose their wider external influence.

7. Discussion of other challenging areas of science

Albert Einstein:

"...I believe in 'Spinoza's God' who reveals himself in the orderly harmony of what exists, not in a God who concerns himself with the fates and actions of human beings..."

The discourse of this book is fundamentally a discussion arising from the results of modern scientific enquiry and the direct conclusions arising from what's transpiring from them. Consistently we are seeing a general rejection of the ideology of naturalism that has developed over the past two to three centuries. This ideology has attached itself to

115

the methodology of science like a limpet mine and yet time after time, modern scientific discoveries are found which commonly refute and countenance naturalist dogma and which clearly do not neatly fit into that worldview. The FTP and QMP are arguably the most robust challenges to this viewpoint (which have been the primary focus of this book), but equally, however, there many other aspects within the broad realm of the sciences which could be mentioned that do not neatly fit into the 'naturalist narrative' either.

The Renaissance scientists were all usually quite religious in persuasion, quite the inverse of the typical modern naturalist/atheist trend and assumption. They sought the 'laws of nature' precisely because behind nature there was thought to be indeed a 'law giver'. The 17th century Dutch philosopher Baruch Spinoza expounded a revised view of God devoid of much of the metaphysical baggaging that can often be associated with religion. Essentially God, for Spinoza, is the impersonal force behind nature which is self-created and controls nature only in the sense of its functionality. This force is entirely abstract from the daily lives, concerns and behavior of human beings, quite contrary to many of the religious views of God. There is no sense to the separation of the 'supernatural and natural' to Spinoza; it either exists or it doesn't. God is the cause of all things; essentially 'God is nature and nature is God'. He was promptly excommunicated as a heretic in 1656 for his troubles.

An obvious counter to this argument is the question why did Spinoza even then use the word 'God' with all its historical associations and baggaging? This is due to the key concept of 'determinism' and 'first cause' that underlined his entire philosophy and worldview. Spinoza identified that a rational viewpoint has to tackle the problem of origin and first cause. In nature everything is caused (determined); there are no real 'coincidences' and indeed there is no real free-will. Therefore, the issue of the 'first cause' always then arises when discussing determinism. From this problem the concept of *substance* is formed, something that purely exists by itself and unto itself and is uncaused by anything else; this is what Spinoza associated with 'God' and felt there was the need to use such a higher term than simply and merely invoking the word 'nature'.

Spinoza is often cited today as a fairly forgotten philosopher, but as science has progressed over the centuries it could be argued the concept of 'Spinoza's God' has become ever more compatible with modern scientific knowledge and the derived understanding, in direct contrast to naturalism.

The next few sections outline some of the other areas of unsolved puzzles in modern science, which are quite distinct from the FTP and QMP problems already discussed previously. These are profoundly challenging to the typical purely naturalist viewpoints that are so often portrayed.

7.1 Darwinian evolution

Wolfgang Pauli

"...in discussions with biologists I met large difficulties when they apply the concept of 'natural selection' in a rather wide field. Without being able to estimate the probability of the occurrence in an empirically given time of just those events, which have been important for the biological evolution. Treating the empirical time scale of the evolution theoretically as infinity they have an easy game, apparently to avoid the concept of purposiveness.

While they pretend to stay in this way completely 'scientific' and 'rational' they become actually very irrational, particularly because they use the word 'chance', not any longer combined with estimations of a mathematically defined probability, in its application to very rare single events more or less synonymous with the old word 'miracle'..."

If the question was asked, 'what are the laws of biology?', what answer would be provided? If in contrast the question was, what are the laws of (for example), logic, physics, astronomy, chemistry, geology, etc., the answer would be very readily and easily provided. Biology, as an academic discipline, is in reality based on comparative evidential and theoretical quicksand and yet is often commonly portrayed culturally as somehow equivalent in authority to the hard sciences.

Darwinian evolution (the theory of natural selection) is often held up as the great 'cornerstone scientific argument' supporting naturalism/atheism, thereby countenancing any possible teleological input into the natural world. The basic premise of the theory of evolution is, of course, entirely sound and well supported by substantial scientific evidence. At least in the sense that it is certain that historically, humans selectively bred domestic dogs from wolves and pigs from wild boars, etc. In the same sense it's clear the external environment acting upon living creatures will also change them over time (albeit likely a slower process). Evidently offspring are not perfect copies of their parents; changes will and do aggregate over successive generations. Darwinism (i.e. the mechanism of natural selection) arguably explains the phenomenon of micro-evolution (changes within a specific species) within living organisms fairly well. Equally, however, it could be argued that much of micro-evolution has more to do with pure random variation as much as any 'naturally selected' input. Micro-evolution in reality involves the long-term loss of genetic information, not gain. A temporary trade off involving the loss of genetic information for opportunistic short-term environmental- based gain by the individual. Those given individuals arguably gain in reality at the long-term genetic detriment of their own species. This in a sense is more 'devolution' than 'evolution'.

But what of the wider claim so often made known as macro-evolution, of 'one distinct species transforming into a distinctly separate other'? Thereby often commonly extrapolated to imply the notion of a 'single common ancestor' of all life? True science (amongst many things) uses very precise language to avoid ambiguities. Pseudoscience, however, has a tendency to deliberately blur concepts using wordplay to create confusion and false equivalence. Evidence for micro-evolution is most assuredly NOT evidence for macro-evolution; they are quite distinct concepts from each other. To give one famous example, a specific species of moth changed its color because of an alteration in its environment (in that case caused by pollution). This, of course, does not provide any evidence whatsoever that you can evolve a fish into an amphibian. Evidently such a small change in a specific species has absolutely nothing to confer about 'one species changing into another'. Let alone has anything to state concerning the unfathomable origin of life or dealing with the immense complexity underpinning biology. Routinely evidence for mere and inevitable micro-evolution is endlessly equated as evidence of the whole supposed subject of evolution, which is clearly disingenuous.

Another good example of this pseudoscience promotion is evidence for the concept known as 'convergent evolution', i.e. such as the Australian Thylacine strongly resembling the unrelated Wolf species, etc. Although the effect is clearly true, this, of course, is an example of the micro-evolutions of two separate species mirroring each other because the undoubted natural forces acting on them are the same. Convergent evolution is again sometimes used disingenuously to falsely conflate truthful evidence for micro-evolution with the supposed occurrence of macro-evolution. Convergent evolution should be really described as the 'parallel micro-evolution' of separate species, because that's what it is.

So what does the theory of evolution really describe? Essentially it is the interaction of an organism's body with the forces of the external environment, thereby impacting on the reproductive success of that organism – either positively or negatively. This notion clearly has very limited explanatory power and is equally very biocentric. Does it really capture and describe any of the underlying complexity of living structures and the origin of the incredible information-storing capacity of DNA? Can its biocentrism explain anything of the pre-biological factors necessarily underpinning the origin of life? Indeed, does an amino acid molecule have a 'body and a reproductive strategy'? How, therefore, can the mechanism of 'natural selection' thereby have any action on an amino acid? How did random natural forces create something of the complexity of DNA from these basic chemicals, particularly if it's unclear how the natural selection mechanism applies to their building blocks in the first place? Can a builder who can't touch bricks build a house? A simple concept stating that when an 'organism survives it survives' is an empty tautology. That hardly captures the immense detail of the underlying chemistry and processes that are required in the first place. Clearly evolutionary theory in terms of 'natural selection' provides very limited detail in attempting to explain any of the origin and complexity of the DNA molecule and the underlying intricate properties of living organisms.

In his book *The Devil's Delusion* David Berlinski outlined that in his view the theory of evolution makes little sense and is supported by little evidence as a scientific theory. But he equally counters that, even if those two premises were true, would you still stop accepting the theory? Many would say no, but the question really revolves around what the true scope and limitations of the theory are (as all theories possess).

What was the title of Charles Darwin's original famous book? The 'Origin of species' – *not* the 'Origin of life'. The concepts of the 'Origin of species' and the 'Origin of life' are very different questions. Darwinists will often claim it an as explanation of both, yet the book attempts to explain the former but has next to nothing to say about the latter. Although recently, Darwinism noticeably seems to be distancing itself from the question of the origin of life /abiogenesis. Progress on the latter question (if there will ever be any) will very much be in hands of rather different areas of science, i.e. complex organic chemistry, (quantum) thermodynamic physics, etc. Indeed, the Origin of Species book does not even contain a single mathematical equation, a noticeable complete and utter lack of any quantitative rigor. Rather unusual in the annals of modern science, to put it mildly.

Many commentators have pointed out that, in fact, biological activity appears to even 'violate' the all-important 2nd law of thermodynamics. Indeed, how do the 'random variations' involved in the so-called natural selection processes ever increase 'observed order and structure'? Unheard of in any other area of science, random variation always, of course, leads to ever greater disorder (entropy). Darwinism, in fact, functions very much in the manner of an old classic 'perpetual motion machine', violating the law of entropy at every step. This is clearly demonstrated by so-called 'genetic computer algorithms' which never appear to generate by themselves any new information. Erwin Schrödinger (in 1944) commented that life must have to utilize 'negative entropy' (negentropy) in order to even function because of its clear apparent violation of the law of entropy – the 2nd law of thermodynamics. Later suggestions, in order to explain this, include concepts such as 'free enthalpy' (also known as 'Gibbs free energy') which would be utilized as critical to life's functioning. Even more exotic suggestions involve the as yet unknown theory of 'quantum-thermodynamics', etc. The main point here being that such discussions of the detailed origin and functioning of biological life clearly have absolutely nothing to do with the simplistic 'Darwinian natural-selection' concept. In countenance to this, the American biochemist Albert Lehninger (1982) argued that the 'order' produced within cells as they grow and divide is more than compensated for by the 'disorder' they create in their surroundings in the course of growth and division. *'Living organisms preserve their internal order by taking from their surroundings free energy, in the form of nutrients or sunlight, and returning to their surroundings an equal amount of energy as heat and entropy.'*

7.2 The karyotype problem

Stephen Jay Gould:

"...when evolutionists study individual adaptations, when they try to explain form and behavior by reconstructing history and assessing current utility, they also tell 'just so' stories - and the agent is natural selection..."

"...virtuosity in invention replaces testability as the criterion for acceptance. ..."

Although it's generally agreed that a hurricane blowing through a junk yard will not create a jumbo jet, the central claim of Darwinian evolution remains that complex structures can be formed by 'slow gradual changes over long periods of time by the process of natural selection'. Though this process may indeed be highly debatable on the grounds of information theory and the law of entropy, is it even known whether it's compatible with the underlying structures of biological life in the first place (as is often assumed)?

DNA within living cells is not held in one single amorphous mass but broken into specific and usually paired discrete objects known as chromosomes (taken from either parent). Different biological species have a clear consistent fixed number, form and structure of chromosomes in their genetic make-up. This is known as the 'karyotype' of the species. An alteration in that count within an individual could only be the result of a spontaneous change at conception within a single generation between certain parents and their specific offspring. How therefore can 'one species change into another' by a process of 'slow natural selection over a long period of time', when by definition such an alteration must occur very rapidly, in the space of a single generation?

However, to be more specific, there are essentially two types of chromosome shift that can occur in living organisms known technically as 'aneuploidy' and 'polyploidy'. Both involve a change in the number/form of chromosomes in the offspring's makeup differing from the parental/species norm. Aneuploidy predominantly occurs in animals and polyploidy predominantly occurs in plants. Aneuploidy is the process in which a given chromosome can either be deleted, fused or duplicated at conception within a given offspring. Polyploidy involves quite a different process, in which there is an increased repetition of chromosome sets within a common set across the whole genome. Going from two pairs, to three pairs, to four pairs, etc.

Although polyploidy is common in, for example, many flowering plants (angiosperms) and can be found to readily form new variants, aneuploidy is indelibly associated with pathology within animals. But where does this lead the Darwinian notion of 'one species turning into another'? Again, we sense instantly the usual pseudoscience tricks at work. They claim that because you can commonly cross two plant 'species' (for example, a cabbage and a turnip) to create a new form (a suede), a genetic mechanism known as polyploidy, that in turn this somehow then automatically implies/proves that within the animal kingdom, you can (for example) turn a frog into a crocodile (supposed genetic mechanism aneuploidy). There is no evidence whatsoever that the undoubtedly pathological mechanism of aneuploidy can achieve any such thing. The method of false-equivalence and misdirection is yet again predictably deployed. Different standards of the word 'species' are being used here to suit the given agenda. If you take the definition of a species as 'the ability to interbreed', then very contradictory standards are being used within the realms of the animal kingdom and the plant kingdom. If turnips and cabbages can readily form offspring, then are they not of the same species? The apparent visual form is of no consequence. Conflicting standards are being applied to suit the underlying narrative. Polyploidy may very well create different variant forms in the realm of plant life, but aneuploidy in the animal world is so obviously associated with clear dysfunction and sickness in the derived individual.

The alteration of a genetic structure (karyotype) is both large and generational. You cannot have a slow stable iterative change in chromosome count over time, i.e. '22.1' chromosomes, smoothly evolving to '22.11' chromosomes, then smoothly evolving to '22.111' chromosomes, etc. You can inherit fragmented sections of a given chromosome (as in the condition known as partial trisomy) but this is a random and damaging process to the organism. Whether either by aneuploidy or polyploidy, there is no slow change in this process. Such a rapid change cannot ever be made consistent with gradualist Darwinian Theory – thereby Darwinian 'inter-special' evolution by natural selection cannot be true. Polyploidy occurs randomly within plants simply because it is genetically possible, not because it was ever 'naturally selected'. Turnips and cabbages have clearly not been made extinct by the derived swede. The swede most definitely does not represent 'Darwinist survival of the fittest' or 'species advancement', genetically speaking, but simply the mere genetic happenstance luck that a polyploidic plant chimera hybrid can be accidentally biologically viable and extant. Equally, aneuploidy occurring by chance within animals is indelibly associated with pathology with the given offspring, hardly qualifying as a 'survival of the fittest' mechanism. Genetic and chromosomal variation is largely based on luck and innate congruence, not by any so-called 'natural selection'.

Examples of the number of chromosomes in specific species:

Common Species Name	Genus and Species	Diploid Chromosome Number
Buffalo	Bison bison	60
Cattle	Bos Taurus	60
Pig	Sus scrofa	38
Sheep	Ovis aries	54
Goat	Capra hircus	60
Horse	Equus caballus	64
Donkey	E. asinus	62
Cat	Felis catus	38
Dog	Canis familiaris	78

Human	Homo sapiens	46
Chimpanzee	Pan troglodytes	48

In the discussion then of the claim of supposed macro-evolution, how could, for example an animal 'species X with 12 chromosomes' transform, therefore, into 'species Y with 14 chromosomes' – by a process of a 'very slow naturally selected change'? Why would thousands/millions (etc.) of individuals within an existing species in the space of one generation all then suddenly and consistently have offspring with the exact same alteration in the number/configuration of their genes and chromosomes to themselves? The number of possible permutations is, of course, enormous in any given change. What conceivable natural explanation or mechanism could there be for such an incredibly unlikely phenomenon? This identical synchronicity in the change would, of course, be totally necessary to retain the reproductive genetic viability of the species.

Alternatively, given a single male and female pair within that species could produce an offspring with a different chromosome count/configuration to the species norm (this clearly has been observed). If so, then how could the specific offspring of a single male and female pair thereby supplant and transmute an entire species? Which, of course, comprises thousands/millions of individuals at any given time. How does a single differing offspring create an entirely new species? Who do they breed with? How/why would they then go on to subsequently generate a new species comprising thousands/millions of commonly genetically distinct individuals? If they could 'back-breed' with one of their original parent species (has been observed), how would the offspring of that one individual and the original species then go on to create an entirely new one? The whole concept is numerically laughable, has never been observed in action and this is aside from discussing the fact that chromosomal changes are indelibly associated with pathology – which is discussed later.

There is no evidence whatsoever that aneuploidy can create new species (at very least within the animal kingdom). Darwinian Theory is incompatible with any such spontaneous change or rapid alteration; everything has to occur as 'very small alterations over a very long period of time' for the theory to even work. The modern scientific concepts of DNA, genes and chromosomes were not understood in Victorian times when Darwin lived and provide a huge problem for the aforementioned theory. The 'quantized' blocky nature of genes, chromosomes, etc. is a very difficult concept for any theory relying on slow gradual change to handle. The usual tactics of evolutionists are to endlessly appeal to 'ever longer periods of time' and 'ever smaller incremental changes' as somehow circumventing the restrictions of the laws of nature – this commonly invoked cop-out most assuredly does NOT work.

Darwinism may explain micro-evolution, but it seriously struggles to explain the mechanism or even demonstrate the possibility of supposed macro-evolution, let alone the origin of life. What demonstrable and documented scientific case evidence exists which exhibits macro-evolution in observed action? What demonstrable and documented scientific case evidence is there of a species (animal at least) ever changing its chromosome count? What demonstrable and documented scientific case evidence is there of a single organism having a different number of chromosomes to its parents and that effect not being associated with some pathology? How does the production of a small number of genetically altered (and damaged) individuals thereby represent the advance of 'survival of the fittest'? It's ironic how Darwinian evolution was unfortunately used historically to justify eugenics and genocide over the course of the past century. In particular when used to justify the sterilization and sometimes even the murder of innocent disabled people, given that the nature of genetic diseases represents one of the strongest refutations of Darwinian evolution.

Some medical conditions being common examples of chromosome alterations in humans include the following (all are associated with pathology to a greater or lesser degree):

- o Turner syndrome (female only – XO)

- o Klinefelter syndrome (male XXY / female XXX)

- o 47, XYY 'Double – Y' syndrome (male only)

- o Down's syndrome #21 Trisomy (both genders)

- o Edward's syndrome #18 Trisomy (both genders)

o Patau's syndrome #13 Trisomy (both genders)

Another good example of a common nonsensical argument used in this area is the often quoted statement that 'chimpanzees and humans share 98% DNA base pairs' (though some studies argue it is more akin to the level of about 70%). Either way, such a lazy equivalence of quantities, of course, proves nothing. For example, a typical motorcar and a typical wind turbine both roughly comprise about 65% steel. They were created for entirely different purposes and the fact they contain similar amounts of a certain base material is irrelevant. Commonality of design/makeup certainly does NOT prove commonality of origin, nor equally does it disprove it either. But evolution endlessly relies on this clearly logically flawed inference. This is a classic example of the oft and commonly seen logically fallacious argument known as 'affirming the consequent'. This is a favorite and routine tactic deployed by the promoters of pseudoscience but is, of course, entirely false in its subsequent claims.

This apparent base-pair similarity, of course, demonstrates in itself fundamentally nothing; we also share 50% of our DNA with a banana – what does the given percentage actually prove? So how then can humans and chimpanzees share a 'common ancestor' when they possess different chromosome counts (48 v 46)? A common evolutionary claim is that human chromosome 2 is the result of the fusion of two simian chromosomes 'accounting' for the chromosome difference between apes and humans. Again, how a species (not an individual) 'achieves' this is not explained; there is no observed scientific evidence of animal species chromosome shift ever being observed, so what is the evidential basis of such a statement? It is claimed human chromosome 2 shows 'internal telomere sequences' that resulted from the supposed fusion, but the purpose of telomeres is to precisely prevent any such fusion. How then did such an unlikely event occur? How did it come to persist in an entire reproductive group of individuals? If in this hypothetical individual two chromosomes did fuse from their 48 chromosome paired parents, then that would leave the other two pairs stranded giving 47 chromosomes, not 46, so then why do humans have a clear identical pair of chromosome 2? What happened to the orphaned pair? Where did the second human chromosome 2 come from when this speculative 47 chromosome ape went on to mate with a normal 48 chromosome ape? Only one human chromosome 2 existed in that pairing. Are they seriously claiming the vanishing unlikely event that the exact same unlikely chromosomal fusing independently occurred in exactly the same place and time between one male and female ape who happened to meet? How can one ape with 47 chromosomes mating with a normal ape with 48 chromosomes supposedly found a new species with 46 chromosomes which now numbers 7.5 billion members?

In addition to this, there is evidence the supposed 'fused telomere sequence' within the human chromosome 2 actually has active genes. This would strongly refute that this area was the result of chromosomal fusing as that area should be completely inert if that was indeed the case.

Recall the famous quote made by Samuel Wilberforce (1805-1873) in the debate with Darwin and Huxley, so often used as a source of ridicule by Darwinists: 'Is it on your grandmother's or grandfather's side that you are descended from an ape?' Actually, when you think in terms of chromosome count shift, Bishop Wilberforce had a rather good point. Obviously, this knowledge was not known at the time, but the above critique in hindsight is indeed rather valid. For evolution to be taken seriously it needs to provide clearly defined mechanistic processes, not this endless web of 'it just so might have it, so it could be true' twaddle. The usual Darwinist trope 'you don't understand the theory' doesn't wash any longer.

Alas, we have yet another evolutionary 'just-so' story lacking real observational support. In contrast, when the extant human Y chromosome is compared to the extant chimpanzee Y chromosome, the result is spectacularly divergent. To such an extent, in fact, that it represents an arguable experimental refutation to one the key claims of evolutionary theory. Remember it is commonly claimed by evolutionists that 'human and chimpanzees evolutionarily diverged about 6 million years ago'. Within the constraints of their own theory, it has been stated the difference in these Y chromosomes would be more on the scale of ~310 million years (i.e. equivalent to the difference on a par with a human and a chicken). Again, the usual evolutionary face-saving 'just-so' stories promptly emerge, claiming that 'chimpanzee Y chromosomes must have lost genetic data at an amazing rate'. Once again, what is the historical evidence for this claim? Why should that be the case in contrast to any other species? Any such stipulation is at best pure conjecture. Different standards are clearly applied to the supposed contentment surrounding the claims around human chromosome 2 'fusing', in stark contrast to the wildly diverging observed reality of the human v simian Y chromosome.

Schematic representations of human and chimpanzee Y chromosomes – showing hugegenetic divergence (2010):

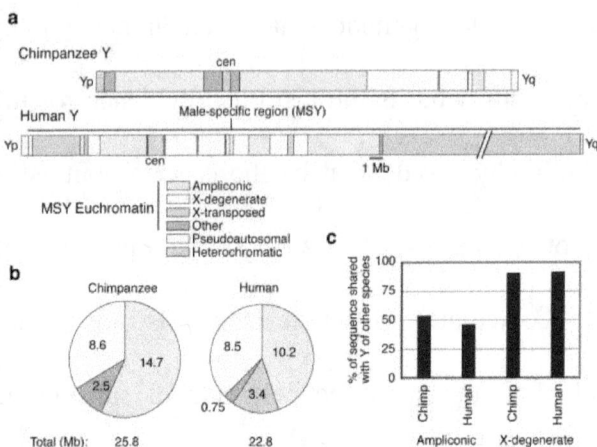

The simplest explanation is usually the correct one and that is that these species emerged independently, the very conclusion that evolutionary pseudoscience spends its whole time desperately trying to avoid. In spite of the ever-burgeoning level of data accruing against it. Are you aware of the Y chromosome issue being particularly popularized by the mainstream narrative? Probably not. Given that data regarding the huge deviation between human and chimpanzee DNA, alongside the general doubt as to whether the

154

Darwinian mechanism of 'decent through modification' can actually even affect a species karyotype – can the notion that 'humans evolved from apes 6 million years ago' truly be honestly defended scientifically? Hominids and apes are separate species. The ancient hominid 'Homo Erectus' is to a modern human what a wolf is to a Labrador dog; both are the product of micro-evolution and nothing else in relation to them has ever been demonstrated.

If macro-evolution can occur in reality (in animals at least), Darwin's 'Theory of natural selection' is definitely NOT the explanation or mechanism behind it. This notion does not in any way claim that chromosome count (karyotype) is equivalent to organism complexity but demonstrates a short-term physical alteration that Darwinian Theory simply cannot handle or be made consistent with.

7.3 The biological chirality problem

Charles McCombs: *"...the fact that chirality was missing in those amino acids is not just a problem to be debated, it points to a catastrophic failure that 'life' cannot come from chemicals by natural processes..."*

Another famous example of modern science not correlating with the 'naturalist agenda' comes this time from the field of biochemistry. The proteins found in biology and our bodies are found to be entirely 'left-handed' as opposed to right-handed. (This is a chemical phenomenon known as chirality or 'handedness'.) Yet when proteins are manufactured in a non-biological context, they are found to be a balanced 50-50 left- and right-handed, as you would arguably expect by natural symmetry. This was famously demonstrated by the Miller-Urey experiment (1953) as shown below and later extended with more sophisticated triggering effects.

Basic diagram of the Miller-Urey experiment (1953):

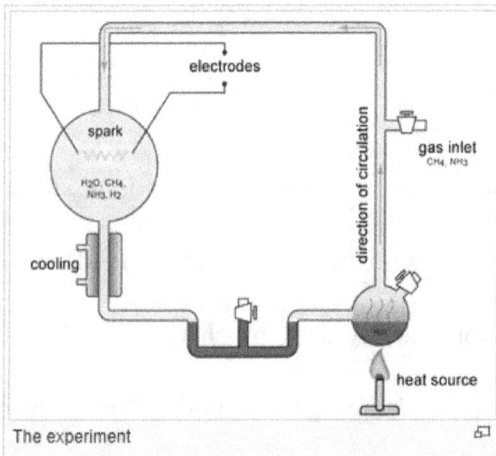

The experiment

The experiment aimed to expose the base chemical to conditions that the early Earth was thought to possess. Such as electrical discharge, UV and volcanic processes. Although the experiment was very effective in producing about 20 amino acids (the base blocks of proteins), the mixture, however, is a balanced 50-50 blend of left and right chiral molecules as already mentioned. Why, therefore, does biological life only use left-handed amino acids when both forms are created equally?

There have been attempts to explain this phenomenon, but none are particularly convincing. Such as the chemical glycine under cool conditions favoring left-handedness in interstellar gas clouds (Don Brownlee, et al); quite how this explains the biological bias on the planet Earth with native 50-50 chiral glycine isn't quite clear. Other 'explanations' include narrow frequency range of circularly polarized UV favoring left-handed molecules (Jeremy Bailey, et al); quite why the frequency range would be limited in the first place isn't clarified. Magnetic field biasing (Eberhard Breitmaier) has also been put forward but the strength of the experimental magnetic field was far higher than that of the Earth's own. Also, the Earth's magnetic field reverses fairly regularly over geologic time, which would continually switch between a left/right bias.

Modern biology, or at least the Neo-Darwinist contingent of it, revolves around the fundamental concept of 'abiogenesis'. Whereas, for example, the real sciences (physics, chemistry, etc.), are based on firm underlying principles underpinned by hard experimental data, biology is based on essentially a myth. Physics is based on hard data and evidence pertaining to the fundamental particles and their interactions (forces) thereof, alongside the Big Bang as the origin and structure-forming event underlying the entire Universe. Likewise, chemistry is based on the atomic chemical elements and the all-important underlying nature of 'chemical-bonds' between them as explained by quantum mechanics, etc. Biology, however, resides on a rather dubious concept known as the aforementioned 'abiogenesis'.

To summarize, 'abiogenesis' is basically the following: 'magic lightning hits some magic sludge in a pond on the surface of the Earth millions of years ago' – and voilà! Proteins, along with the most complex construct in the known Universe (the DNA molecule), magically appear instantly!! There's absolutely no scientific data or detailed explanation of that process, of course, and it has never been reproduced or explained whatsoever, but you're not allowed to mention that fact.

Every experiment including and since the Miller-Urey onwards has put common electricity through a chemical mix and (unsurprisingly) generated a certain 50-50 mix of right/left chiral molecules (as expected due to natural balance/symmetry). So how then does every amino acid inside every living being on Earth comprise entirely charily left-handed molecules only? That's a great deal of biomass. So what makes the 'magic lightning in the past' of abiogenesis so extra special when standard electricity used in laboratories today can only ever produce a mere subset of the required amino acids which are evenly 50-50 charily mixed right and left?

In addition to this, it also should be noted that the original experiment actually got the chemical mix representing the early Earth's atmosphere completely wrong. When the gases were updated with the correct mix, the experiment produced essentially nothing. Another criticism is the level of particular design involved with the apparatus. Does that really represent the 'uncaused natural/environmental mechanisms' that it claims to signify?

The Miller-Urey experiment and later experiments like it were meant to show the possibility of life forming by natural processes but ultimately achieved the total opposite – demonstrating the essential experimental impossibility of so-called abiogenesis. Not only can 'abiogenesis' not describe the origin of life, or the immensely complicated origin of DNA and the immense complex underlying systems that underpin life, but nor can it explain the chiral bias found in all living organisms. So why then is life chirally 'left-handed'? No serious naturalist answer has been ever provided.

But, of course, according to biologists in the converse, any discussion of intelligent design is clearly 'entirely irrational and silly'.

Abiogenesis (like Darwinism) is, of course, based entirely on faith, faith that one day 'a great breakthrough' will be found, whatever that 'great breakthrough' is. Curious is it not then, how they are forever attacking people who hold to religious faith whilst their own concepts are based on pure quicksand.

7.4 Darwinian evolution (Continued)

Charles Darwin:

"...why then is not every geological formation and every stratum full of such intermediate links?

Geology assuredly does not reveal any such finely graduated organic chain; and this perhaps is the most obvious and serious objection which can be urged against my theory..."

The notion that 'one species can transform into another separate species' is little more than a Victorian myth – that we've all been systematically indoctrinated to accept as 'unequivocal truth'. This is at least true in the animal kingdom, but that is more than sufficient for the point of argument. Specific species can micro-evolve over time constrained within their own karyotype, but the occurrence of macro-evolution is arguably physically and genetically almost certainly impossible. It has never been directly observed in nature to occur or replicated in the lab; the fossil record utterly refutes it and it is arguably genetically improbable to impossible (aneuploidy) – hardly qualifying as 'unquestionable truth', do you not think?

Yet Darwinists, however, in their haughty arrogance and questionable scientific rigor, generally perform every pseudoscience trick in the book, every word game and every possible subterfuge to avoid any recognition of the clear and enormous conceptual and functional difference between micro-evolution and macro-evolution (the boundary being alterations in the species karyotype, not some arbitrary line). They are only too well aware that the moment that they concede any difference between micro-evolution and macro-evolution is the self-same moment that the Darwinist worldview dies. They retain a deliberately vague and flawed definition of the word species precisely to circumvent the clear difference between the two. A species is defined by its karyotype, which is what gives it its form, reproductive viability and overwhelmingly its genetic health. Any karyotype alteration is routinely observed to lead inexorably to a certain degree of pathology and infertility and in many circumstances even death. Equally you cannot assert 'evolution is about changes in populations rather than individuals' as is sometimes heard to be claimed. You cannot magically separate a 'population' from its individuals; its individual reproductive pairs are what constitute the population and keep it viable. (This is why healthy societies treat the nuclear family with such great reverence, but that's for another discussion.)

Indeed, it could be argued that aneuploidy, as a process by design within DNA, is an innate mechanism that functions precisely to prevent any such so called macro-evolution speciation from actually occurring (again certainly true in animals at least). The fundamental aspect is this: a genetic/karyotype altered individual does not go on to spawn a new distinct species, in spite of the claims made about it. That is precisely what needs to happen, of course, to allow macro-evolution to occur, thereby generating the so called interlinked 'tree of life' from a 'single common ancestor'. You cannot even produce a stable sub-species from mixing animals as similar as a horse and a donkey. Mules can be formed as one-offs but are almost always infertile; those exceedingly rare examples that are fertile have always been female with only around 60 known cases globally in the past 500 years. With only one known recorded account of a hinny giving birth in modern times being in China in 1981. In addition, many of those exceptionally rare births actually reproduced more horses or donkeys as offspring. The point is if evolution is true, it should not be this difficult to create new species. It should occur very readily, and the fossil record should be jam-packed with examples of it – it isn't. You do not readily find transitional forms in the fossil record simply because they do not exist; they likely never have and never will. Equally, visit radiation-affected zones in places such as Hiroshima, Nagasaki and Chernobyl and count all the 'new life forms' now present; you won't find many. The main species lines of life on Earth were all created independently by a mechanism unknown and have either micro-evolved/sub-speciated over time or gone extinct. There is no real evidence to support the concept of a 'single common ancestor' or the 'tree of life', certainly as depicted by Darwinists. The mechanism of micro-evolution will function exactly the same whether life started once, twice or a billion times. Not only is there no physical evidence for a 'single common ancestor', nor is there any theoretical requirement for it either. The 'single common ancestor' concept is a completely unnecessary postulate that functions only as an article of faith for atheists. The 'tree of life' concept simply follows on its coattails.

With evolution, we see an endless popularized cultural overstretching of the theory into all areas of science, as though a simplistic theory of biology has anything to comment upon in relation to the fundamental sciences. Darwinian Theory has nothing to say about most areas of science: geology, chemistry, physics, the quantum measurement problem, and ultimately the finely tuned laws of physics, etc. When any idea is pushed beyond the limits of its applicability it becomes misguided. If a 'theory about human emotions', for example, was put forward based on the theory of gravity (akin to such historic notions of astrology and lunacy), the argument would appear rather flawed. There is nothing silly about the theory of gravity, of course; it remains one of the pinnacles of human intellectual achievement. But any notion pushed outside its natural boundaries then enters the realm of at best pseudoscience and more likely pure nonsense. Too often the Darwinist Theory of natural selection is pushed way outside its explanatory power; again it remains a narrow theory of micro-evolutionary speciation and yet provides no convincing mechanism for supposed 'macro-evolution' (if even possible) and no description or detail of the origin of life. If (for example) the theory could explain the origin of the DNA molecule, then it would already have done so, as the aforementioned theory already exists. It is very unusual to hold out for a scientific theory to suddenly start explaining phenomena in the future that it cannot do so already; its explanatory power is fairly self-contained at conception. What 'big new discoveries' are Darwinists exactly holding out for? The fact, of course, that the origin of DNA to this day remains a complete mystery demonstrates that all extant current theories (obviously including Darwinian Theory) are clearly deficient. Making such claims then is, therefore, mere faith-based nonsense. An alternative theory known as 'Punctuated Equilibria' has actually been suggested in contrast to traditional Darwinism. This is the notion that species hardly alter over geologic time (stasis), but occasionally change rapidly due to rare geological changes creating sub-groups through isolation. Arguably, this functions, in fact, as a good, usable model of sub-speciation within the species karyotype envelope, even if the notion of macro-evolution is rejected.

A good example of the endless over-stretching of the theory is the example of the long-claimed fossil of Archaeopteryx (once dubbed the 'first bird') being heralded as a 'great example of an evolutionary transitional form'. As modern science demonstrates, Archaeopteryx is in reality a very unremarkable example of a run of the mill feathered theropod dinosaur, albeit the Berlin specimen is a very nice fossil. In fact, the evidence suggests that most theropod dinosaurs possessed feathers (many including flight feathers). Indeed, even a large animal such as Tyrannosaurus Rex is also now commonly regarded to have had downy feathers running along its back. Archaeopteryx is not a transitional form; it is a feathered dinosaur. Birds are simply a subtype of theropod dinosaur and are not a different separate species from them. Modern birds evolved from their Mesozoic ancestors and are fundamentally of the same form as them. An example of strong micro-evolution in action perhaps, but that is clearly not evidence for macro-evolution. The rapid dubbing of Archaeopteryx as 'the first bird' on such flimsy evidential grounds (basically because it was discovered early on) is a perfect demonstration of the over- eagerness and lack of caution and rigor within the subject of biological evolution. One of the key hallmarks, it has to be remarked, of pseudoscience.

Archaeopteryx – 'Once dubbed the first bird': Long vaunted as an example of an 'evolutionary transitional form' – which is highly debatable in modern science.

The clearest criticism of evolution theory of all is in terms of exactly what the falsifying aspects of the various points of the theory are. What measurements could be made that might refute the idea, thereby making it a robust scientific theory? There is an element of 'anything fits' and 'everything goes', in spite of a lack of detail within the theory of Darwinian evolution. What isn't it claimed to explain popularly (e.g. DNA, etc.)? That's a great weakness, not a strength. The chronic lack of 'evolutionary transitional forms' in the fossil record (the pre-Cambrian era in particular) could be mooted as a falsifying prediction of the theory, which could in turn be taken to give it some scientific credence but that at the same time is hardly a verification of its claims. The pre-Cambrian period should be jam-packed with 'evolutionary transitional forms' in order to account for the subsequent 'Cambrian explosion' in complex life forms. In reality the pre-Cambrian is utterly barren and dead, a complete observational refutation of Darwinian evolution. Going back in time, supposed transitional forms should be thoroughly ubiquitous within the fossil record. Totally outnumbering the 'familiar forms' many times to one. Indeed, the further back in time you go, the familiar forms should evaporate altogether. The total opposite is observed; species appear to emerge in the fossil record as fully formed, whilst familiar forms stretch way back in geologic history virtually unchanged to their modern form. Above all, the total absence of clear transitional forms is astounding if you honestly still believe in macro-evolution. Many species have gone extinct for granted, but certainly that's no evidence for macro-evolution. Overall, the chronic lack of observed transitional forms in the fossil record, after nearly two centuries of the scientific discipline of paleontology, demonstrates the unlikeliness of macro-evolution from even occurring.

In reality, biology has no explanation for the origin of life (abiogenesis) and can provide no explanation or mechanism to justify the concept of inter-speciation (macro-evolution). Given there are roughly 8.7 million (eukaryotic) species on Earth, the total lack of any observational evidence in support of macro-evolution or any replication of it in the laboratory represents a huge problem. As described earlier, there is little scientific basis to the notion of a 'single universal common ancestor' or the 'tree of life' so often popularly suggested. The evidence would arguably rather suggest that life formed independently many times on the Earth by a mechanism unknown, whose environment is indeed so uniquely suited to support biological life.

Stark contrast between the 'tree of life' prediction of Darwinian evolution and the observed fossil record:

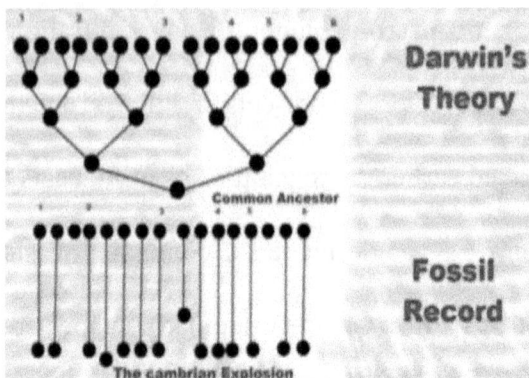

Evolutionists, of course, strongly dislike that notion as it ramps the impossible probabilities of life occurring even higher. They can just about justify in their mindset the naturalistic impossibility of life occurring once, but not more. Indeed, the desperate fallback concept of 'transpermia' (the notion that life fell out of the sky one day – as an explanation for the existence of life on Earth) becomes ever more popular amongst evolutionists. There is no way the supposed 'Darwinist natural-selection mechanism' can possibly alter a species karyotype makeup in a manner that it remains reproductively viable. How can a process so indelibly associated with pathology possibly be the engine of the 'progress of living species'? How can a chromosomally altered individual found a new species? Macro-evolution is nonsensical. Equally, the supposed concept of abiogenesis cannot handle or resolve the chirality problem (amongst other things). These discoveries demolish the many naturalist arguments which are so often portrayed as 'signed and sealed scientific facts' in this area.

The honest view of the author is that if Charles Darwin was alive today, he would utterly reject his own theory; he himself in his own lifetime stated the many possibilities that would derail his theory – much has been discovered since. In reality, Darwin's 'Theory of evolution by natural selection' is little more than a 19th century gradualist relic, which is incompatible with the blocky 'quantized' nature of DNA and hence base amino acids, genes, chromosomes, etc. It would be greatly beneficial to the subject area of biology if Darwinian evolution was to be consigned to the history books, in the manner which physicists dispensed with much of the prior gradualistic classical physics over a century ago.

The questions of both the origin of a life and the origin of species remain an entirely unsolved scientific problem. There is no technical explanation available at this time. How life formed, how the different species came into existence and the comparative utter lack of evidence for life elsewhere in the solar system, remains a great unsolved mystery.

(In addition, also refer to Appendix 2 for a classic case study of scientific fraud).

7.5 The consciousness problem

Max Planck

"...I regard consciousness as fundamental. I regard matter as derivative from consciousness.

We cannot get behind consciousness. Everything that we talk about, everything that we regard as existing, postulates consciousness..."

Many naturalists still cling to the notion that the nature of consciousness will one day be biologically determined. After many years of cutting up brains one day a 'great breakthrough will suddenly occur' even though consciousness remains a total mystery biologically. It is often claimed 'consciousness emerges from chemical reactions in the brain' but you'd need to understand the functioning of consciousness to possibly make such a claim. What experimental result demonstrates a chemical basis to consciousness? The firing of neurons responding to external stimuli does not represent consciousness. A computer stores data on its hard disks and has executed processes ('thoughts') in its CPU currently running in its RAM chip ('memory'), but a computer is clearly not conscious. The fact that the brain has been shown to be compartmentalized into specific faculties is not an explanation of consciousness. The removal of external sensory input from your senses into the brain does not render you non-conscious. As many philosophers in history have pointed out, you cannot look into your own eyes without a mirror, you cannot bite your own teeth, you cannot taste your own tongue, and you cannot touch your own finger with that finger. Consciousness is vastly more than mere simple biological feedback.

Fundamentally, the epistemological Achilles heel of atheism is the following – if your brain is merely a bag of chemicals formed as a result of random natural forces, then why do you possess so much faith in your own power of reason? Reason being typically seen as the cornerstone of conscious thought. What gives you your confidence in your own 'intellectual prowess' (and others') if it's the result of mere random uncaused irrelevant events? Reason is, of course, entirely based on faith, faith that reason itself has any value and accuracy within itself – and on what *is* that based exactly? Clearly a self-defeating and circular argument from the atheist's own viewpoint. Where does the authority/accuracy of your 'human reason' come from? At least religious people own up to the reality of faith common to them and atheists in equal measure.

Another issue as mentioned previously is that it's experimentally proven that information can travel at infinite speed; if it were constituted of matter or energy, it would be strictly bounded by the speed of light. If consciousness is based on pure information (as suspected), it cannot therefore be in any way material in nature. Consciousness acts upon the matter/energy within the brain, not the other way around.

From the realm of physics, the results of modern quantum mechanics and the delayed choice eraser experiment (DCQE) in particular put a profound spin onto the notion of biocentric consciousness. The results of the DCQE experiment suggest two critical things about reality:

1. Consciousness cannot be removed from the behavior observed in the experiment. Consciousness observation changes reality.

2. Only the present moment possesses any certainty and the past can be altered to be consistent with the present moment (retro-causality).

This would seek to suggest that consciousness is, in fact, more fundamental than matter and therefore matter cannot be the fundamental source of consciousness. This presents a major problem for naturalism as can be discussed from the two key points.

Premise 1 – consciousness solely arises from biological brains:

In view of the results of DCQE experiment this represents a major paradox. For matter to exist in any certain form consciousness observation is required, but if consciousness solely arises from biological brains, then they would never have existed in the first place in order to become conscious.

Premise 2 – consciousness is more fundamental than matter:

Here there is no innate paradox as consciousness is taken to be independent of matter and the observed results would then logically follow – as long as a 'conscious observer' is on hand to undertake the experiment.

However, the philosophical sting in the tail is very clear. In order to resolve either premise there is by consequence the unequivocal need for a universal, non-biological, pre-existing consciousness to 'lock' matter into a definite form in the first place. This again is a major scientific challenge to any naturalist explanation, which clearly points to a theistic explanation and signifies teleological influence upon nature supported by experimental data.

7.6 The matter/anti-matter symmetry problem

Thomas Kuhn:

"...the history of science indicates that, particularly in the early developmental stages of a new paradigm, it is not even very difficult to invent such alternates. But that invention of alternates is just what scientists seldom undertake except during the pre-paradigm stage of their science's development and at very special occasions during its subsequent evolution. ..."

It's been calculated that the chance of our Universe being in the 'low entropy state' observed as it is now, is the mind-boggling probability value of $10^{10^{132}}$ to 1. This refers to the tremendous degree and unlikely level of ordered structure to be seen in the visible Universe on all length scales. This number even makes some of the fine-tuning values stated previously seem mundane (see also Appendix 1). There are many such similar problematic concepts in the realm of physics and cosmology.

One particularly challenging problem worth discussing is a simple but major scientific problem in the inability to find any explanation for the asymmetry in the amount of matter and anti-matter in the early Universe. This presents a real problem, as therefore no material should exist at all given it would be completely annihilated by the equal 50-50 amounts of both forms. This would therefore result in absolutely no material particles existing in the Universe whatsoever in order to create atoms, chemistry, etc. Thereby yielding no stars, galaxies or planets and therefore definitely no life. No explanation for this has yet been found.

Some may try and label such statements as the 'god of the gaps' concept. However, there is no 'gap' in dealing with absolutely fundamental and ubiquitous phenomena. These effects have a bearing not only on the existence, but also the behavior of every single entity in the Universe, hardly the realm of 'gaps and exceptions'.

8. Summary

Robert Jastrow:

"...for the scientist who has lived by his faith in the power of reason, the story ends like a bad dream. He has scaled the mountains of ignorance, he is about to conquer the highest peak; as he pulls himself over the final rock, he is greeted by a band of theologians who have been sitting there for centuries..."

Science is not the neat process it is sometimes portrayed as, and many problems remain within most fields of science. Indeed, as many philosophers over the years have pointed out such as George Berkeley (1685-1753) and also similar ideas later echoed upon by Thomas Kuhn (1922-1995), science tends to hold to a current paradigm of dogma which is widely taught, and then, occasionally, a revolution in the subject occurs (a 'paradigm shift') and a whole new dogma arises to take its place. The basis of science upon repeatable tested experiment is its great strength. However, the validity of the many theories and axioms of science are nowhere near as solid as some like to portray. True science is based on statements which can be fully tested experimentally and are critically falsifiable, as described brilliantly by the works of Sir Karl Popper (1902-1994). A theory in which everything goes, anything goes, and everything fits, regardless of what's measured, is utter worthless garbage. This is the dreaded world of pseudo-science, which is a fairly common phenomenon currently.

When a scientific field which is backed by a huge amount of experimental data which in turn has survived endless falsification testing (such as the FTP and QMP) is perceived to be sidelined, it is a clear demonstration of the dogma within science. Those who endlessly hold out for new results which will 'dispel the conclusions' of the FTP and QMP rather than accepting them as the current paradigm (which is what they are) are taking a very strange position for a 'rational scientist'. This is simply a faith- based position taken because the conclusions of what science is now actually describing are not seen as palatable to the naturalist narrative. The ideology of naturalism is therefore held way above the experimentally attested science within the modern academic community. What, therefore, is the motivation of such a position? It's entirely equivalent to the so-called 'irrational position' of religious thought that they are so quick to denounce.

The study of the origin of the Universe inevitably possesses some of the most fundamental questions that can be raised. The default position for science should always be 'agnostic' with any concept/theory being required to withstand an immense level of evidence-based testing as means of its possible falsification.

The evidence of modern physics and cosmology inexorably points towards either a theistic or solipsistic view of the origin of nature with little room for other positions. The results of the QMP resoundingly dismisses a realistic/materialistic view of nature; the FTP in turn profoundly displays a Universe which (at the cosmological level at least) was indeed intelligently designed at its formation. Do the concepts of the 'fine-tuner' and the 'cosmological observer' sound consistent with a naturalistic/atheistic explanation of nature?

The flow and orientation of modern science is actually very much against the tide of naturalism and atheism seen in much of modern culture, contrary to what is often portrayed. Those who seek to lazily conflate science with naturalism and atheism are in fact on very questionable scientific and philosophical ground indeed. All roads lead to the same place if they are rooted in truth; the fact that science and religious tradition so often strongly concur in spite of being such diverse wisdoms should not be a surprise.

9. Afterword

St. Thomas Aquinas:

"...to one who has faith, no explanation is necessary...

...to one without faith, no explanation is possible..."

The modern world seems to be under the grip of a truly great intellectual and mindful malaise. The great modern phenomenon of social media certainly appears to be demonstrating this effect. The world now seems to be full of experts on everything and anything. Let alone in the popular realms of politics and society, but also in science, religion, theology and the 'great cause of environmentalism'. Many post views on social media about various subjects based on next to little to no knowledge, so they can garner (for example) their 'Facebook Friends' to approve with their many likes, such that they can apparently 'confirm' their newly found views. Truly the most flawed and biased of peer review mechanisms possible. Social media has become a giant global exercise in the fallacy of induction, with ever more entrenched groups preaching to their own choir and excluding all others.

Although the focus of this book is entirely concentrated on scientific research and is definitely not a book about religion, it would be unfair not to mention some of its theological implications and in particular to the FTP/QMP concepts. The primary aim was to outline some of the many fields of modern scientific research to open-minded people, which most definitely do not tally with the supposed 'neat and closed' secular, naturalist, materialist and often atheist sentiments of much of modern culture.

People can often be heard to ask, 'Do you believe in God?' This makes it sound as if you really have a choice; there is no choice in rationality. Rationality is entirely involved in the question of what is true and what is false. Although truth is a very difficult thing to uncover with certainty, there is no choice involved of any kind. You have no choice but to accept the abstract concept of God (the 'fine-tuner'/'cosmological observer') because the hard scientific evidence entirely supports a 'finely-tuned/observed' Universe. Therefore, you have no choice but to accept the then implied 'fine-tuner/observer'. In the same way the theory of Electromagnetism which implies the highly abstract concept of 'electric charge', gravity implies the highly abstract concept of 'mass-energy', the strong nuclear force that implies the highly abstract concept of 'color-charge', etc.

You're welcome to believe, if you like, that when freely dropping a stationary object 'it will not fall'. It, of course, always does fall, but you're entitled to your false belief. Belief has nothing to do with rational understanding; the object always falls because gravity is, in fact, the result of the 'implied existence of mass/energy'. Again, indeed electromagnetism is the 'implied result of the abstract concept of electric charge', the strong nuclear force of the 'implied result of color charge', etc.

The observed effect entirely implies the source concept and to doubt hard evidence is the epitome of being irrational. The hard, experimental data underpinning the FTP and the QMP problems entirely compel you to accept the existence of God. But, of course, you're welcome to being an atheist, but do not ever fool yourself that you are being 'rational' in that view.

The Universe we know only exists because God finely tuned it to take the form that it does. The Universe is only stable and extant because of the endless fixed observation upon it by the omniscient presence of God. Consciousness creates matter, not the other way round. Biology is simply a footnote. To hold any real confidence in the power of intellectual reason you really have to accept the immaterial basis of consciousness (which originates in God).

For the past couple of centuries, we've had a plethora of so-called 'philosophers and writers', whose primary aim has been to denigrate the concept of God and religion. Often using dubious interpretations of science as a countenance to a lesser or greater degree. A perfect example being the works of Nietzsche who famously derided Christianity as a 'doctrine for the weak'. Just as Karl Popper demolished Marxism, directly citing how the observation and flow of history completely falsify Marxist theories and its claims, such a similar observation of history could equally be made against Nietzsche. It is clear when European countries were strongly Christian, they were at the peak of their power historically, not only in terms of military and economic dominance but also their internal social and political stability. As Christianity has been chipped away over the decades, these countries have descended into ever greater weakness and social division. Hardly a confirmation of Nietzsche's claims; strength comes from moral self-control and certainty, in alignment with the pursuit of knowledge. Emotions such as envy (so lauded by Nietzsche) are poisonous mis-directions of the weak minded. Nietzsche was a pathetic failure as a man and is one of those classic so-called 'thinkers' who primarily wished to propagate his own low standards onto everyone else, whilst attacking and undermining the moral establishment that possessed real strength.

Nietzsche's ideas directly fed into Nazism, Marx's into Communism. Between them, these 'atheist ideologies' have resulted in the estimated deaths of about 120 million innocent people in the course of the last century alone (and that doesn't include a single solider killed in war). Amazing, isn't it then, how till this day, so many people are quick to defend and promote the 'ideas and concepts' of this pair of atheist fools.

Atheists generally love to consider themselves to be 'intelligent, informed and good honest moral people'. Yet to be an atheist is to be a moral relativist; it goes with the territory. Without a higher authority, of course, all ethical values are mere fickle human opinion blowing in the wind like a leaf (to and fro). You always know an atheist when you meet one; the underlying sanctimonious smugness, the moral dissonance, the fake sense of self superiority, etc. Yet they're all too well aware that in themselves deep down, they know that they

pertain to no fixed values or constraints. That they

can switch their opinions on a sixpence and

comfortably hold the most ridiculously

contradictory views in the self-same moment.

There's pure anarchy in the eyes, minds and words

of these people (I know, I used to be one).

10. Appendix 1

The following describe a list examples of the Finely Tuned parameters described qualitatively, known to operate within the Universe:

- The strong nuclear force constant:

  If larger: no hydrogen would form; atomic nuclei for most life-essential elements would be unstable, therefore no chemistry or life.

  If smaller: no elements heavier than hydrogen would form: again no chemistry or life.

- The weak nuclear force constant:

  If larger: too much hydrogen would convert to helium in big bang; hence, stars would convert too much matter into heavy elements making life chemistry impossible.

If smaller: too little helium would be produced from big bang; hence, stars would convert too little matter into heavy elements making life chemistry impossible.

- The gravitational force constant:

  If larger: stars would be too hot and would burn too rapidly and too unevenly for life chemistry.

  If smaller: stars would be too cool to ignite. Nuclear fusion; thus, many of the elements needed for life chemistry would never form.

- The electromagnetic force constant:

  If greater: chemical bonding would be disrupted; elements more massive than boron would be unstable to fission.

If lesser: chemical bonding would be insufficient for life chemistry.

- The ratio of electromagnetic force constant to gravitational force constant:

  If larger: all stars would be at least 40% more massive than the sun; hence, stellar burning would be too brief and too uneven for life support.

  If smaller: all stars would be at least 20% less massive than the sun, thus incapable of producing heavy elements.

- The ratio of electron to proton mass:

  If larger: chemical bonding would be insufficient for life chemistry.

  If smaller: same as above.

- The ratio of number of protons to number of

  electrons:

  If larger: electromagnetism would dominate

  gravity, preventing galaxy, star, and planet

  formation

  If smaller: same as above.

- The expansion rate of the universe:

  If larger: no galaxies would form.

  If smaller: universe would collapse, even

  before stars formed.

- The entropy level of the universe:

  If larger: stars would not form within proto-

  galaxies.

  If smaller: no proto-galaxies would form.

- The mass density of the universe:

  If larger: overabundance of deuterium from big bang would cause stars to burn rapidly, too rapidly for life to form.

  If smaller: insufficient helium from big bang would result in a shortage of heavy elements.

- The velocity of light:

  If faster: stars would be too luminous for life support.

  If slower: stars would be insufficiently luminous for life support.

- The age of the Universe:

  If older: no solar-type stars in a stable burning phase would exist in the right (for life) part of the galaxy.

If younger: solar-type stars in a stable

burning phase would not yet have formed.

- The initial uniformity of radiation:

  If more uniform: stars, star clusters, and

  galaxies would not have formed.

  If less uniform: Universe by now would be

  mostly black holes and empty space.

- The average distance between galaxies:

  If larger: star formation late enough in the

  history of the Universe would be hampered

  by lack of material.

  If smaller: gravitational tug-of-wars would

  destabilize the sun's orbit.

- The density of galaxy cluster:

  If denser: galaxy collisions and mergers

  would disrupt the sun's orbit.

  If less dense: star formation late enough in

  the history of the Universe would be

  hampered by lack of material.

- The average distance between stars:

  If larger: heavy element density would be

  too sparse for rocky planets to form.

  If smaller: planetary orbits would be too

  unstable for life.

- The fine structure constant (describing the

  fine-structure splitting of spectral lines):

  If larger: all stars would be at least 30% less

  massive than the sun.

If larger than 0.06: matter would be unstable

in large magnetic fields.

If smaller: all stars would be at least 80%

more massive than the sun.

- The decay rate of protons:

  If greater: life would be exterminated by the

  release of radiation.

  If smaller: universe would contain

  insufficient matter for life.

- The 12C to 16O nuclear energy level ratio:

  If larger: universe would contain insufficient

  oxygen for life.

  If smaller: universe would contain

  insufficient carbon for life.

- The ground state energy level for 4He:

  If larger: universe would contain insufficient carbon and oxygen for life.

  If smaller: same as above.

- The decay rate of 8Be:

  If slower: heavy element fusion would generate catastrophic explosions in all the stars.

  If faster: no element heavier than beryllium would form; thus, no life chemistry.

- The ratio of neutron mass to proton mass:

  If higher: neutron decay would yield too few neutrons for the formation of many life-essential elements.

  If lower: neutron decay would produce so

many neutrons as to cause collapse of all

stars into neutron stars or black holes.

- The initial excess of nucleons over anti-

  nucleons:

  If greater: radiation would prohibit planet

  formation.

  If lesser: matter would be insufficient for

  galaxy or star formation.

- Polarity of the water molecule:

  If greater: heat of fusion and vaporization

  would be too high for life.

  If smaller: heat of fusion and vaporization

  would be too low for life; liquid water

  would not work as a solvent for life

chemistry; ice would not float, and a runaway freeze-up would result.

- Supernovae eruptions:

  If too close, too frequent, or too late: radiation would exterminate life on the planet.

  If too distant, too infrequent, or too soon: heavy elements would be too sparse for rocky planets to form.

- White dwarf binaries:

  If too few: insufficient fluorine would exist for life chemistry.

  If too many: planetary orbits would be too unstable for life.

  If formed too soon: insufficient fluorine

production.

If formed too late: fluorine would arrive too late for life chemistry.

- The ratio of exotic matter mass to ordinary matter mass:

If larger: Universe would collapse before solar-type stars could form.

If smaller: no galaxies would form.

- The number of effective dimensions in the early Universe:

If larger: quantum mechanics, gravity and relativity could not coexist; thus, life would be impossible.

If smaller: same result.

- The number of effective dimensions in the present Universe:

  If smaller: electron, planet and star orbits would become unstable.

  If larger: same result.

- The mass of the neutrino:

  If smaller: galaxy clusters, galaxies and stars would not form.

  If larger: galaxy clusters and galaxies would be too dense.

- Big Bang ripples:

  If smaller: galaxies would not form; Universe would expand too rapidly.

  If larger: galaxies/galaxy clusters would be too dense for life; black holes would dominate; Universe would collapse before

life-site could form.

- The size of the relativistic dilation factor:

  If smaller: certain life-essential chemical

  reactions will not function properly.

  If larger: same result.

- The uncertainty magnitude in the

  Heisenberg uncertainty principle:

  If smaller: oxygen transport to body cells

  would be too small and certain life-essential

  elements would be unstable.

  If larger: oxygen transport to body cells

  would be too great and certain life-essential

  elements would be unstable.

- The cosmological constant:

  If larger: Universe would expand too

  quickly to form solar-type stars.

11. Appendix 2

Haeckel's Embryos - A classic case study of scientific fraud and the promotion of pseudoscience:

One of the biggest sources of scientific misinformation in relatively modern times is known as the case of 'Haeckel's Embryos', published by German biologist Ernst Haeckel between 1868 and 1908. Haeckel popularized a series of faked illustrations of the embryological stages of vertebrates, in order to propagate the agenda of Darwinian evolution to the wider public which were widely used in education. The images are still well known today and are often still perceived as being accurate, sadly fooling many even to the present day (including for a long time the author of this book).

The premise was to overly highlight similarities between species at their formative stages and massively conceal their huge differences at the same time; the depictions are highly inaccurate. Haeckel's aim was to convince the reader that all vertebrates share a common ancestor (remains an unproven concept), as he described it himself, *'Ontogeny recapitulates phylogeny – our embryonic development repeats our evolutionary past.'*

An example of Haeckel's deliberately misleading and highly inaccurate 'Embryo diagrams', designed to promote evolutionary pseudoscience:

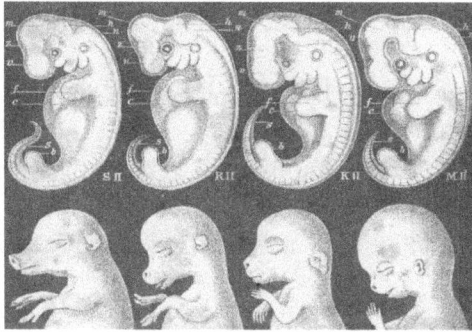

In comparison, modern photographic data:

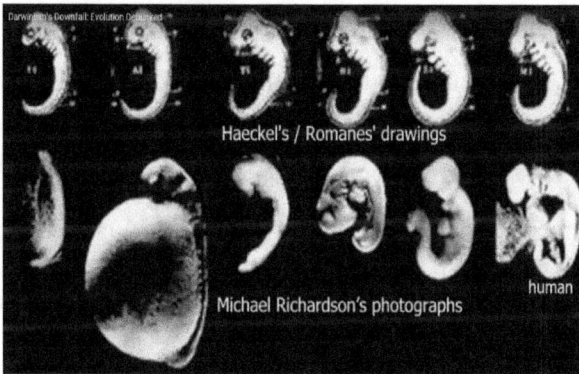

Haeckel's / Romanes' drawings

Michael Richardson's photographs

human

In reality the development of different species even during their early stages are observed to be significantly different. Greatly reflecting the fundamental separate nature of species, underlying their deep essential differences such as chromosome

225

count. This represents arguably one the most prevalent and effective pieces of pseudoscience propaganda ever published. Apparently even Scott F. Gilbert authored a book as recently as 1985, a developmental biology textbook, inadvertently using Haeckel's images.

Real science is based on falsifiable testable predications made against real world data. The fact certain proponents of evolutionary theory have felt the need to make the use of such unscientific propaganda in an attempt to justify its claims, is self-explanatory.

12. Glossary

Brief summary of key terms used in the book:

Affirming the consequent – Describes a common logically fallacious statement of the converse or confusion of necessity and sufficiency. Is a formal fallacy of inferring the converse from the original statement.

For example, 'My driveway is wet, so it must be raining' is an example of this fallacy (someone may have turned on a hose). The fallacious statement is based on the true statement that 'if it is raining, then the driveway is wet', but is a fallacy because the order of cause and effect have been reversed.

Aneuploidy – The genetic presence of an abnormal number of chromosomes in a cell.

Atheism - The belief that there is no God, or the denial that God or gods exist.

Anthropic Principle - The anthropic principle is a philosophical consideration that observations of the Universe must be compatible with the conscious and sapient life that observes it.

Big Bang (The) – The rapid expansion of matter from a state of extremely high density and temperature which according to current cosmological theories marked the origin of the Universe.

Biology – The study of living organisms, divided into many specialized fields that cover their morphology, physiology, anatomy, behavior, origin and distribution.

Cambrian (and pre-Cambrian) – The Cambrian period (541 million BC) marked the beginning of the more complex life forms. Little is known about the pre-Cambrian period although it consists of nearly seven-eighths of the Earth's history.

Chirality – Asymmetric in such a way that the structure and its mirror image are not superimposable. Chemical chirality, more specifically, is a geometric property of some molecules and ions. A chiral molecule/ion is non-superimposable on its mirror image. The presence of an asymmetric carbon center is one of several structural features that induce chirality in organic and inorganic molecules.

Chirality Problem (The) – In living organisms, the observed fact that the amino acid molecules within living organisms on Earth all possess left-handed chirality. If life is the result of 'uncaused small random fluctuations (natural-selection) over a long period of time', then surely they should possess a 50-50 mix of left- and right- handed molecules, but this is universally observed not to be the case.

Chromosome Count Problem (The) – See the Karyotype Problem.

Color Charge – A property of quarks and gluons that is related to the particles' interactions by the strong nuclear force in the theory of quantum chromodynamics (QCD). This color charge differs from electromagnetic charges since electromagnetic charges have only one kind of value.

Convergent evolution – The independent evolution of similar features in species of different lineages. Convergent evolution creates analogous structures that have similar form or function but were not present in the last common ancestor of those groups. The cladistic term for the same phenomenon is homoplasy.

Cosmology – The science of the study of the origin and development of the Universe. Modern cosmology is dominated by the Big Bang theory, which brings together observational astronomy and particle physics.

Cosmological Constant (The) – Originally introduced into the theory of General Relativity by Albert Einstein (in 1917) as an additional effective 'fudge-factor' to keep the Universe in a balanced 'steady state' (manifesting as an extra factor being a constant multiple of the metric tensor added into the main field equation). Later experimentally discovered (1998) to be a definite physical constant from the study of distant supernovas, and whose value has since been accurately experimentally measured. This demonstrated that the expansion of the Universe is actually accelerating rather than slowing as opposed to what was expected under gravitational breaking.

Deductive reasoning – Contrasts with inductive reasoning in the following way: in deductive reasoning, a conclusion is reached reductively by applying general rules which hold over the entirety of a closed domain of discourse, narrowing the range under consideration until only the conclusion(s) is left. In inductive reasoning, the conclusion is reached by generalizing or extrapolating from specific cases to general rules, i.e., there is epistemic uncertainty. However, the inductive reasoning mentioned here is not the same as induction used in mathematical proofs – mathematical induction is actually a form of deductive reasoning.

Determinism – The philosophical theory that all events, including moral choices, are completely determined by previously existing causes. Determinism is usually understood to preclude free will because it entails that humans cannot act otherwise than they do. The theory holds that the Universe is utterly rational because complete knowledge of any given situation assures that unerring knowledge of its future is also possible. Determinism is often contrasted with free will.

Determinism (Causal) – Slightly distinct from above, causal determinism in physics is also known as cause-and-effect. It is the concept that events within a given paradigm are bound by causality in such a way that any state (of an object or event) is completely determined by prior states. This is the diametric opposite to the concept of retro-causality which is suggested by certain experiments in quantum physics.

Electric Charge – A physical property of matter that causes it to experience a force when placed in an electromagnetic field. There are two types of electric charges: positive and negative (commonly carried by protons and electrons, respectively). Like charges repel and unlike attract.

Epistemology – Study of the nature of knowledge, justification, and the rationality of belief. Much debate in epistemology centers on four areas:
(1) The philosophical analysis of the nature of knowledge and how it relates to such concepts as truth, belief, and justification

(2) Various problems of skepticism

(3) The sources and scope of knowledge and justified belief

(4) The criteria for knowledge and justification.

Epistemology addresses such questions as:

'What makes justified beliefs justified?'

'What does it mean to say that we know something?'

and fundamentally 'How do we know that we know?'

Eukaryotic (Life) – A domain of organisms having cells each with a distinct nucleus within which the genetic material is contained. Generally associated with the more 'complex lifeforms', eukaryotes include protoctists, fungi, plants and animals.

Fine-Tuning Problem (FTP) – The observation from modern fundamental physics and cosmology that the values of the many fundamental constants are mutually set in such a fashion to allow highly complex structures to exist in the Universe on all length-scales. The tiniest deviations from these values would consistently result in the Universe consisting of significantly less order and complex structures. The probability of a Universe existing in which something as complex as biological life could form naturally, with all its myriad of pre-dependencies by chance, is vanishingly small.

Fundamental Constants – Many concepts and relationships in physics require specific constant terms in equations which have to be experimentally determined. These usually denote specific properties of certain particles or their laws of interaction. Generally nothing can determine these values theoretically and they have no effect on the behavior and form of the equations of physics other than defining the relative strength of interactions. The reason for the actual quantities values take is entirely unknown.

General Relativity – (GR, also known as the general theory of relativity or GTR) is the geometric theory of gravitation published by Albert Einstein in 1915 and the current description of macroscopic gravitation in modern physics. General Relativity generalizes Special Relativity and Newton's law of universal gravitation, providing a unified description of gravity as a geometric property of space and time, or space-time. In particular, the curvature of space-time is directly related to the energy and momentum of whatever matter and radiation are present. The relation is specified by the Einstein field equations, a system of partial differential equations.

Gravity – The force that radially attracts a body towards the center of the earth, or towards any other physical body having the property mass.

Hubble Flow – The discovery that all galaxies appear to be moving away from each other and the speed is proportional to the distance. Such behavior is indicative of an explosion and by clear implication the Universe had a definite temporal origin.

Idealism – Things exist only as ideas in the mind rather than as material objects independent of the mind.

Inductive reasoning – A method of reasoning in which the premises are viewed as supplying some evidence for the truth of the conclusion, this is in contrast to deductive reasoning. While the conclusion of a deductive argument is certain, the truth of the conclusion of an inductive argument may be probable, based upon the evidence given.

Karyotype Problem (The) – Each living species has a consistent fixed number of chromosomes in its genetic makeup (its karyotype). For this number to change can only be the result of a spontaneous single-generation alteration occurring between the parents and their certain specific offspring. How can therefore 'one species evolve into another' by a process of 'slow natural selection over a long period of time', when such a change can only occur within a single generation?

Realism – The theory that physical objects continue to exist whether they are perceived or not.

Many-worlds interpretation of quantum mechanics (The) – One interpretation/explanation of the phenomena of quantum mechanics in which 'choice-points' cause the Universe to split into many parallel existing time streams; all possible outcomes became manifest. This is taken as the main rival to the 'Copenhagen interpretation'. The key aspect here is understanding this explanation is based entirely within our Universe and pertains entirely to the same Big Bang and its finely tuned laws of nature; it's simply a description of how this, our single Universe, functions. Importantly, this concept has absolutely nothing to do with the often-discussed concept of the 'Multiverse'.

Macro-evolution – The supposed change from one distinct separate species into another, which has never been observed or measured in action.

Materialism – The philosophic doctrine that matter is the only reality and that everything in the world, including thought, will and feeling, can be explained in terms of matter alone.

Micro-evolution – The gradual change within a distinct species sometimes also forming sub-species, this can occur naturally or by man-made selective breeding (such as dogs).

Miller-Urey Experiment – This was a chemical experiment that simulated the conditions thought at the time to be present on the early Earth and tested the chemical origin of life under those conditions. The experiment supported Alexander Oparin's and J.B.S. Haldane's hypothesis that putative conditions on the primitive Earth favored chemical reactions that synthesized more complex organic compounds from simpler inorganic precursors. The experiment is thought to have synthesized about 20 amino associated with life.

Considered to be the classic experiment investigating abiogenesis, it was conducted in 1952-3 by Stanley Miller, with assistance from Harold Urey, at the University of Chicago and later the University of California, San Diego and published the following year.

Modern Physics – Generally defined as Physics discovered post the year 1900 with the advent of the work of Max Planck. This, in particular, encompasses the revolutions of Quantum Mechanics and General Relativity and generally denotes the demarcation with the prior era of classical physics which emerged in the Renaissance era.

Monism – The doctrine that the person consists of only a single substance, or that there is no crucial difference between mental and physical events or properties.

Multiverse – A speculative notion that other 'universes' could exist independently of our known Universe. These 'universes' consisting of a separate formation event and possessing different physical laws, number of spatial dimensions, etc., there is no real theoretical reason to suppose and absolutely no evidence to support such a claim. Very importantly, this is not to be confused with the 'many-worlds' interpretation of quantum mechanics, which is a totally different concept.

Naïve Realism – The doctrine that in perception of physical objects what is before the mind is the object itself and not a representation of it.

Naturalism – An ideological account of the world in terms of the causes and natural forces that rejects all spiritual, supernatural or teleological explanations. This is taken to run in parallel to the methodology of science.

Occam's Razer (The Law of Parsimony) – The philosophical concept that the simplest explanation usually tends to be the right one. In other words, when presented with competing hypothetical answers to a problem, one should select the answer that makes the fewest underlying assumptions and avoids unnecessary complexity that offers no additional explanatory power.

Paradigm Shift (also 'radical theory change') – A concept identified by the American physicist and philosopher Thomas Kuhn (1922-1996), it is a fundamental change in the basic concepts and experimental practices of a scientific discipline. Kuhn contrasted these shifts, which characterize a scientific revolution, to the activity of normal science, which he described as scientific work done within a prevailing framework (or paradigm). In this context, the word 'paradigm' is used in its original Greek meaning, as 'example'.

Polyploidy – The state of a cell or organism having more than two paired (homologous) sets of chromosomes.

Punctuated Equilibria – A theory in evolutionary biology in contrast to traditional Darwinism, which proposes that once a species appears in the fossil record the population will become stable, showing little evolutionary change for most of its geological history (stasis). When significant evolutionary change occurs, the theory proposes that it is generally restricted to rare and geologically rapid events of branching speciation called 'cladogenesis'. Arguably a good usable model of sub-speciation within the species karyotype envelope even if the notion of macro-evolution is rejected.

Quantum Measurement Problem (QMP) – The measurement problem in quantum mechanics is the problem of how (or whether) wave function collapse occurs. The inability to observe this process directly has given rise to different interpretations of quantum mechanics and poses a key set of questions that each interpretation must answer. The wave function in quantum mechanics evolves deterministically according to the Schrödinger equation as a linear superposition of different states, but actual measurements always find the physical system in a definite state. Any future evolution is based on the state the system was discovered to be in when the measurement was made, meaning that the measurement 'did something' to the system that is not obviously a consequence of Schrödinger evolution.

Various different concepts have been introduced in an attempt to explain this phenomenon. The main ones being as follows: the Copenhagen interpretation, Hugh Everett's 'many-worlds' interpretation, the De Broglie–Bohm theory and the Ghirardi–Rimini–Weber (GRW) theory.

Quantum Mechanics – The branch of mechanics that deals with the mathematical description of the motion and interaction of subatomic particles, incorporating the concepts of quantization of energy, wave–particle duality, the uncertainty principle, the exclusion principle and the correspondence principle.

Rational Theism – The concept that scientific evidence does imply the existence of a God, in the context of an external agent independent to and being the designer/creator of the Universe (no religious connotation).

Schrödinger Equation – A differential equation which forms the basis of the quantum-mechanical description of matter in terms of the wave-like properties of particles in a field. Its solution is related to the probability density of a particle in space and time.

Special Relativity – (SR, also known as the special theory of relativity or STR) is the generally accepted and experimentally well-confirmed physical theory regarding the relationship between space and time. In Albert Einstein's original pedagogical treatment, it is based on the two following postulates:

The laws of physics are invariant (i.e. identical) in all inertial systems (i.e. non-accelerating frames of reference).

The speed of light in a vacuum is the same for all observers, regardless of the motion of the light source.

Solipsism – The view or theory that the self is all that can be known to exist. The existence of separate external minds to the self is denied.

Supernatural (of a manifestation or event) – Attributed to some force that is beyond a scientific understanding or the known laws of nature.

Telomere – Is a region of repetitive nucleotide sequences at each end of a chromosome, which protects the end of the chromosome from deterioration or from fusion with neighboring chromosomes.

Theism – The belief in the existence of a God or gods.

Thermodynamics – The branch of physical science that deals with the relations between heat and other forms of energy (such as mechanical, electrical or chemical energy) and (by extension) of the relationships between all forms of energy.

Transpermia (also Panspermia) – The concept that life originates from outside the Earth in the interplanetary medium and fell to the Earth in the manner of dust and meteorites.

This is taken as an explanation for the existence of life on Earth but still provides no mechanistic explanation of the origin of life, how life can survive the vast amounts of time in the harsh solar/cosmic environment and how delicate biological systems can survive entry into the Earth's atmosphere. The apparent sterility of the other planets in contrast to Earth is another problem, in particular Mars which is also in the sun's habitable zone.

13. Index

'Allegory of the cave', conjecture, 63

Abiogenesis, 144-7, 219

Alan Aspect, 66

Albert Einstein, 66,67,70,104

Anthropic Principle, 25, 58

Aristotle, 41,62

Atheism, 6, 11, 12, 18, 19, 25, 30, 111, 166, 176, 177, 205

Atheist, 12, 18, 88

Bertrand Russell, 93

Big Bang, 29, 34

biology, 11,12, 39, 52, 59, 92, 96, 110, 113

Boëthius, 98, 99, 100, 101

Charles Darwin, 117, 148

chirality, 141, 162

Chromosome Count Problem, 207

Chromosomes, 121, 122, 125, 126, 127, 129, 133, 134

Color charge, 81, 181

Consciousness, 21, 23, 89, 90, 91, 92, 96, 164-8

Cosmological constant, 28, 55

Cosmological observer, 71, 81, 83, 84, 89

Cosmology, 10, 18, 20, 21, 30, 31, 171, 176

Darwinist evolution, 10

David Berlinski, 116

Delayed choice quantum eraser, 67

DNA, 115, 116, 121, 129, 132, 133, 139, 145

Edwin Hubble, 28

Electric charge, 80, 81, 82

Entropy, 51, 118, 119, 121

Erwin Schrödinger, 45, 118

Eugene Wigner, 61

Free will, 100

Fine-tuner, 81, 82, 84

Fine-Tuning Problem, 20, 31, 52

Fred Hoyle, 29, 52

FTP, 20, 31, 32, 34, 52, 53, 54, 58, 59, 60, 73, 74, 75, 77

Fundamental constants, 53

General Relativity, 28

George Berkeley, 148

God, 7, 23, 25, 32, 58, 60, 71, 73, 79, 80

Hubble flow, 28, 29

Ibn Sahl, 46

Idealism, 24, 62, 215

James Clerk Maxwell,

80

Johannes Kepler, 43

Karl Popper, 14, 22, 174,

183

Many-worlds'

interpretation, 224

Material reality, 57, 62

Materialism, 24, 30, 61,

218

Metaphysics, 27, 72

Miller-Urey experiment,

142

Modern physics, 20, 26

Monism, 26, 61, 220

Multiverse, 58, 59, 74,

75, 76

Naïve Realism, 24, 70,

220

Naturalism, 12, 13, 18,

19, 21, 24, 26, 30,

104, 107, 111, 168,

175, 176, 177, 220

Naturalist, 11, 12, 18, 27,

30, 88, 105, 108, 141,

147, 160

Occam's razer (the Law

of Parsimony), 78

Paradigm shift, 174

Physics, 10, 12, 20, 31,

33, 34, 38, 39, 50, 52,

53, 59, 60, 78, 80, 82,

85, 110, 144, 153

Plato, 62, 65

Ptolemy, 46

Pythagoras, 32, 35

QMP, 20, 31, 61, 64, 73,

81, 83, 84, 89, 91, 98,

105, 175

Quantum Measurement

Problem, 20, 31, 61

Quantum mechanics, 20,

31, 45, 61, 63, 66, 70,

72, 82, 91, 99, 217

Realism, 24, 70, 216

Robert Jastrow, 173

Saul Perlmutter, 55

Schrödinger equation, 91

Sir Isaac Newton, *6*, 61

Solipsism, 23, 30, 61, 71,

93, 94, 95, 226

Special relativity, 67

Spinoza, 104, 105, 106,

107

St. Thomas Aquinas, 75,
80, 178
Steven Weinberg, 74

Supergravity, 39

Supernatural, 19, 25, 106,

Superstrings, 39

Theism, 25, 30

thermodynamics, 38, 39,

49, 118

Thomas Kuhn, 170, 173

Universe, 9, 11, 16, 18,
19, 22, 23, 25, 27, 28,
29, 30, 31, 32, 34, 37,
48, 53, 54, 55, 56, 57,
58, 59, 60, 62, 63, 65,
71, 73, 88, 144, 170, 18

About The Author

Duncan Kilburn holds a bachelors and masters degrees in Physics along with a Doctor of Philosophy degree in Meteorology.

In view of this particular book, the author feels more recourse to the often described 'new atheism' movement (as coined by the journalist Gary Wolf in 2006) over the last few decades is long overdue and will assist in bringing more balance to the debate.

About The Publisher

L.R. Price Publications is dedicated to publishing books by unknown authors.

We use a mixture of both traditional and modern publishing options to bring our authors' words to the wider world.

We print, publish, distribute and market books in a variety of formats including paperback and hardback, e-books, digital audio books and online.

If you're an author interested in getting your book published; or a book retailer interested in selling our books, please contact us.

www.lrpricepublications.com

L.R. Price Publications Ltd.,
27 Old Gloucester Street,
London, WC1N 3AX.
020 3051 9572
publishing@lrprice.com

9 781838 061081